I0503927

MISSION: HR

LOOKING FOR CLARITY

MISSION: HR
Looking for Clarity

Denis W Barnard

Copyright © 2023 by Denis W Barnard
All rights reserved

Contents

INTRODUCTION

I work in Human Resources (HR). There, I said it. And I'm sure many of you reading this will know all about the pitying looks and flippant jokes that result from that statement.

I've been in HR for forty years, starting in 'Personnel' as it was then, as a greenhorn from the Accounts Department with zero knowledge. My predecessor had done the job for 32 years, and sitting with him in the handover period, I was struck by how peaceful everything was. One month later, I was sitting at that desk on my own and the phone never stopped ringing.

After serving my time at the corporate 'coal face' I went independent and have served about the same number of years as an independent consultant, working with enterprises of various sizes and sectors across international boundaries.

The Human Resources department is pretty much the biggest target in the sights of every employer and every employee. It carries the can for everything that goes wrong: Redundancy, Sickness absence, poor Performance, and toxic Culture. It also picks up every crappy job that's going in an effort to prove its value.

Much blame is, in truth, laid at the wrong doors, but Human Resources inadvertently take the rap because they pride themselves on being the 'heart and soul' of the organisation. Hence a treadmill of headlines in the industry press along the lines of: "Inflation: What HR must do" or "Employees unhappy: HR must act now".

My decades of working in HR and observation of many HR departments led me to conclude that:

- it means something different to every organisation
- HR's current activities are extremely broad in scope
- many HR departments are engaged on doing things that add little or no value in real terms.

I've heard and read many opinions on HR's purpose from people both inside and outside of the profession, and I have drawn heavily on these to draw a picture of how things stand right now. The extracts shown are by no means definitive but are meant to give a flavour of what's talked about. What they do have in common is that they are almost always inaccurate, although like most fallacies they contain more than a grain of truth.

These pages certainly aren't meant as some quick 'blueprint for success', but rather to define what I call 'the true mission of HR', which needs to be distilled from the tangle of activities that comprise it at present and instead aligned far more closely with the business and its aims. As you read through, you will notice that I have quoted extensively from sources where I agree with their way of looking at things and dealing with them. I've never been in the business of 're-inventing the wheel', and those sources are more knowledgeable than I am in their specific areas. If I can help some HR colleagues whack through the weeds that are choking the garden of our profession, then mission accomplished.

If I appear at times over-critical of the function, this is not intentional, but we really need face up to things as they are, or we'll never change them for the better.

The world of HR is a fascinating one, and this together with my involvement with the HR technology industry have permitted me over time to meet and work with some exemplary members of the HR and wider business communities who remain as trusted friends and colleagues to this day. Their contribution to this work is immeasurable.

I would also like to thank the very special quartet of my peers who gave of their valuable time to read through the drafts and give crucial commentary and encouragement.

MISSION: HR

PART ONE – THE STATUS QUO

Chapter One – What is HR?

The functional title 'Human Resources' is surely ready for changing and I'll be looking at that in Chapter Nineteen.

Meanwhile, 'Human Resources' shows two sides of the same coin, either 'our people are our greatest asset' or 'salary costs are our greatest overhead' depending on what side of the balance sheet you happen to stand.

Here's a **CIPD (Chartered Institute of Personnel and Development)** definition of the HR function:

> *"Through the people professionals who work within it, the HR function helps an organisation deliver its corporate strategy and objectives by effectively recruiting and developing people and managing their performance. HR objectives are delivered differently in different types of organisations."*

SHRM (Society for Human Resource Management) explains it thus:

> *"Human resource management (HRM) is the process of managing an organization's employees. HRM includes all aspects of people management to effectively meet an organization's goals."*

Both are sufficiently broad in scope as to give different interpretations depending on who reads them, so one aim of this book is to throw some light on the salient points of the HR mission.

It's also amusing to look at definitions that we pulled from **OpenAI** in December 2022 when we put two questions to it:

"What is human resources?"

> *"Human Resources (HR) is a term used to describe the department or division of a business that is responsible for managing and helping the organization's employees. This includes the recruitment, hiring, training, and performance management of staff, as well as the development of policies*

and procedures related to payroll, benefits, and other employee-related activities."

"What are the main human resources activities?"

"1. Recruiting and Hiring: Developing job descriptions, selecting candidates, conducting interviews, and onboarding new employees.

2. Performance Management: Setting goals and objectives, evaluating performance, and providing feedback.

3. Employee Relations: Handling grievances, investigating complaints, and fostering a positive work environment.

4. Compensation and Benefits: Establishing salary structures and benefit plans, administering payroll, and overseeing employee incentives.

5. Training and Development: Identifying training needs, designing and delivering training programs, and tracking employee development.

6. Compliance: Ensuring that HR practices comply with local and federal laws and regulations.

7. Employee Engagement: Developing strategies to increase employee engagement and morale."

As we examine various aspects of these definitions, I will be explaining where I am not in agreement and why.

At this point, I will introduce a list of statements that I maintain that HR **isn't**, using some general comments that I hear and read all the time, occasionally from HR people, and quite a lot from articles in the general media.

HR makes the organisational policies and rules

HR may help present the statutory legal requirements of employment law in the organisation, but the rules are set by management. So, if the rules say you can't take more than two weeks' holiday at any one time, that's a company requirement, and just because it appears in the Employee Handbook doesn't mean that HR cooked it up, it was more likely based on requirements from operational departments.

HR is the employees' advocate

No, Unions and Works councils are examples of employee advocates. I truly think that this is where a lot of misunderstanding arises, as, from what I read almost daily quite a few HR people think that they are there to support the workforce in disputes.

Every organisation should have a proper laid-down procedure for grievances, discipline and appeals and both employees and managers should be fully aware of those procedures and encouraged to follow them.

This, I should emphasise, is an important area for HR to be communicating.

In many situations HR has a crucial part to play in the employment relations process and they will contaminate those processes by getting involved as the first port of call for complaints which should more properly be taken up elsewhere.

Many tribunal cases are launched because the organisation's managers fail to follow their own rules, and many get thrown out because the employee failed to follow the laid-down procedure.

HR must lose this 'tea and tissues' image to which everyone runs with a problem.

HR is about managing the people and hiring and firing them

The only people that HR should be managing, and firing, are HR people, not anybody else's. HR may be involved in redundancy exercises to ensure compliance, but that's about it.

Line management are responsible for hiring and firing, although HR should be responsible for making sure that they are trained to do it correctly and compliantly, as we will see later.

One activity that eats HR time and resources in many outfits is the practice of having an HR representative attend every candidate interview, for whatever reason. Yes, it's still a widespread practice, believe it or not, although HR know next to nothing about the job, what is required or the relevant departmental culture.

Anything additional that needs to be known about the terms and conditions of employment can easily be attached to an email.

HR is responsible for employee performance

The only performance that HR is responsible for is that of the HR department, not any other department. HR has no first-hand knowledge of individual or departmental performance other than that provided by line management.

HR will almost certainly have performance statistics captured in an HR system, but these are for use by management for a variety of purposes.

Note: With the above two points, I am already at odds with both the **CIPD** and **SHRM** descriptions, which state that part of the function is managing employees or their performance.

HR is responsible for absence levels in the organisation

HR is not responsible for levels of sickness in the organisation, but they will be responsible for the procedure.

Often used as an HR metric, there is little or no line of sight between HR activity and sickness absence. Although they shouldn't claim credit for reductions, they certainly cannot be blamed if there is a 'flu epidemic that loses numbers of working days.

Some HR departments operate a 'return to work' interview system, which is intended to reduce the number of casual days taken off by individuals, but looked at broadly, the major causes of absence are stress, workplace injury and musculoskeletal disorders (*Source: Labour Force Survey*), the latter two of which can be reduced by preventative measures.

Workplace stress causes can be more difficult to separate from more general lifestyle causes, but it would be true to say that having good quality trained line management would help to alleviate the problem.

Sources:
https://www.hse.gov.uk/stress/causes.htm
https://www.hse.gov.uk/statistics/dayslost.htm

HR takes the lead on organisational culture and morale.

Job titles such as Head of People and Culture are becoming more commonplace, yet although the HR department may be symptomatic of an organisation's culture, there's no getting away from the fact that Culture starts at the very top.

If the head of the fish is rotten with bullying, harassment, expenses fiddling and blame apportioning, then these become acceptable norms throughout.

The state of organisational morale reflects the workforce's views of this type of culture. People either hunker down or leave when they realise that their work is directed by people they cannot respect or even trust.

Even the most brilliant HR people cannot effectively counteract egregious management behaviour, but then again, they should always stand up against it, and not just bend with the prevailing wind as has happened far too often in the past.

Culture won't be created by putting 'motivational' posters on the walls, framing optimistic mission statements in Reception or even appointing a 'Chief Happiness Officer'.

HR organises Christmas parties and social events (and wraps all the presents.)

I shouldn't really have to comment on this, but I know it still happens.

At an event some time back, a colleague and I met the Head of HR of a well-known UK airport with over 500 employees. As my colleague had a total of three HR people for 750 employees, we were interested to hear how many strong her HR department was. Eighteen.

We were dumbstruck. My colleague then said that maybe that number could be trimmed somewhat, the Head of HR said there was no way, otherwise who would wrap the staff presents and organise social events!

In my own experience, I once observed the entire HR department of a company, from the Director downwards, engaged for nearly a whole day boxing up wine for staff gifts, an activity that should more properly have been delegated to the supplier.

HR administers pension funds, medical insurance, and car fleets.

Because these are 'people benefits' it is generally assumed that HR should be charged with the administration of them, and certainly in previous times HR was happy to take these on to try to prove its value to the employer.

Nowadays, this work is seen as an obstacle to progression, and that much more of the burden should either be extensively automated or driven by the actual providers liaising directly with the employee.

Conclusion

The lack of clarity both within and outside the department has resulted in HR taking on irrelevant activities – generally work that no-one else wants to do. Ironically, in time these activities go on to form a comfort zone, resulting in HR's apparent permanent state of firefighting, and of course, firefighting is a good explanation for missing deadlines and not making expected progress.

Between what people think HR does but doesn't, and the things that HR does but shouldn't, there's not a lot of space to be effective – or appreciated. It all results in a sort of functional inferiority complex.

It's no wonder so many HR professionals report being stressed, demotivated and unappreciated; they are operating predominantly in a vacuum.

Chapter Two – The HR Business Partner (HRBP)

In 1997 **Dave Ulrich** published the '**Human Resource Champions'** book that helped to define the HR business partner in terms of roles and outcomes within an organisation.

In more recent times he commented:

"In the ensuing 20 years, much has changed in the world of technology; and much has changed in the world of HR. The business partner concept has dramatically evolved."

"HR's evolution will continue as current business issues place HR centre stage (e.g., digital information age, #MeToo movement) and HR needs to continually upgrade to respond;"

Source:
https://strategicleaders.com/evolution-hr-business-partner/

The initial model split HR into four sections:

'Strategic Partner

To help manage the development and growth of the workforce. They look to the customer to see what they could make better, and they review the systems and processes that might help to deliver what the customer wants and needs more efficiently.

Administrative Expert

Who has more of an internally focused role. They manage costs, people, and the overall delivery of the day-to-day 'business as usual' output

Change Agent

Looking into the company's overall culture and thinks about how it can be better, both from a personal and professional perspective. They'll connect with line managers to lead and facilitate change to make the organization a better place for everyone

Employee Champion

Aids employees to speak up and ensures they feel heard and

respected at work. They support the delivery of processes and practicalities that ensure safeguarding, and they can also help to make sure the company's people are happier and healthier, which is of huge overall benefit to the organization.'

Source:
https://www.testcandidates.com/magazine/the-david-ulrich-hr-model/#:~:text=What%20is%20The%20David%20Ulrich,way%20of%20organizing%20HR%20functions

There is no doubt that the HRBP model gave definition to HR activities at a critical time, and from that point it has been widely accepted by HR and beyond.

You will see later that the 'Employee Champion' role has been taken rather too literally by some HR people who interpret that as 'Employee Advocate' which is something very different.

The 'Administrative Expert' description is far too vague; 'managing costs and people' is wide of the mark, especially as HR only manages HR people. Administration as an activity is – or should be -dissolving in the face of automation, so we can see this part of the equation will disappear over time.

'Strategic Partner and Change Agent' demand a business background and mindset that is probably beyond many HR practitioners at the outset and remember that to achieve any type of change takes credibility at the highest level.

In February 2021, Lucy Adams CEO of DisruptiveHR wrote a post entitled 'The New HR Business Partner' outlined the multiple challenges of the job, the required results, and attributes likely to be present to be able to do the job. I've had had plenty of comments from business people over the years that HR all too often appears to be an obstacle to Change!

She went on to say that:

"What is perhaps less well understood is what it takes to be an exceptional, high performing HR Business Partner....In our experience many organisations find that there is still a way to

go before the role of HR Business Partner is operating as they would like."

Source:
https://disruptivehr.com/the-new-hrbp/

This is interesting, as there is always an assumption in business models that designated staff can actually do the job.

Chris Roebuck, writing in **PeopleSpace**, averred that the HRBP is only a step in a journey towards greater organisational success. He listed five weaknesses of the HRBP model, being:

*"**Capability shortfalls***

The implementation of the HRBP role often reveals critical shortfalls in key areas needed to be effective, in particular around how good is the HRBP's understanding of the real drivers of organisational success and how forward-thinking is the HRBP

Reactive not proactive

The HRBP usually exists to serve the client, ie the internal customer, but all too often that means waiting for the client to approach them rather than taking an active approach

Not focusing on real value because of unaligned requests

There is a risk that the client's requests are based on activity that is not aligned to the strategic goals. Therefore the HRBP will be doing work that is unaligned to strategic objectives. This, says Roebuck, could be up to 25% of what the HRBP is asked to do. "HRBPs are being dragged down into the grass and not focusing on things that add real value because the client is not asking for them," he says

Assumed not real need

There can be an assumption about what needs to be done rather than what the real need is. Take projects. An HRBP may take the project in isolation, so when it fails that HRBP will look at the reasons behind the failure for that individual project. Yet only about 30% of initiatives are ever effectively implemented. The

HRBP needs to look at the symptoms across the business rather than taking an isolated view.

Inappropriate solutions

There is a tendency to give the internal customer 'best practice'. This is not always what the customer needs or wants. Instead HRBPs should be delivering best current outcome."

Here again we see the capability question raised. An article in **HR Magazine** in March 2017 claimed that "*HR business partner models fail to add strategic value*"

It went on:

"While HRDs generally have good business knowledge those lower down are failing to add value.

HR business partner models are failing to add strategic value to businesses, according to a Henley Business School report seen exclusively by HR magazine.

Andrew Mayo, professor of human capital management at **Middlesex University** and co-author of the HR with Purpose: Future Models of HR report, said that many business partners (BPs) are underprepared to view the business strategically.

"In my view, the CIPD wants business partners to be strategic but it doesn't train people to provide that," he said. "The top levels of HR understand the business well, but the levels further down do not know how to contribute."

Part of the problem, the researchers argue, comes from patchy implementation of the recommendations of various theorists, such as Dave Ulrich...

Kathryn Pritchard, group chief people officer for **Odeon UCI Cinemas** Holdings, suggested that the implementation of the Ulrich model does not always present opportunities for BPs to add value. "The effectiveness of the BP model, like lots of things in business, depends on the capability of the BPs and the context they work in," she told HR magazine. "Sometimes it adds value and sometimes less so.

"Where I have seen it add less value is where HR models have evolved very strategic and commercial centres of excellence and have evolved their analytics function. When both of these are working well, and alongside an efficient 'business as usual' transactional arm, there is less opportunity for BPs to add strategic value."

Mayo added that in some cases BPs do not have the time or energy to offer a strategic contribution. "You see this where the HR department has been cut down to the bone," he said. "There's simply not the capacity to do anything other than the transactional. There's not enough time to be strategic too."

When approached by HR magazine Ulrich responded quite correctly that "while implementation can sometimes be behind the failings, this does not mean the model is flawed." "Like using the full services of a smartphone, you cannot blame the phone for bad apps when the users do not know how to use them."

Instead businesses should be adapting the partner model. "HR structure should match business structure," he explained. "We argue that emerging HR practices should be aligned, innovative, integrated, and simplistic."

"However, the report suggests that other areas of the business do not view HR in a positive light, which could be hampering partnering. The research cites 2016 research from **Bersin**, which found that while 29% of those in HR class their performance as below adequate, 38% from other areas of the business believe they are under-performing. Similarly, while 39% of HR staff believed they were good or excellent, only 28% from those outside HR agree."

"Mayo suggested that HR professionals and aspiring BPs could learn to become a better partner to the rest of the business by spending time in another function. "A six-month secondment in another area of the business will provide a different perspective," he said.

Pritchard added: "I think we as HR professionals need to develop critical expertise about organisation performance and *capability and then bring that to life in new and creative ways for the businesses we work in. Great BPs should be leading their businesses in understanding how to achieve optimal organisation performance, developing a sense of where value is being created and lost in a business, and finding ways to increase value as core parts of the role."*

Source:
https://www.hrmagazine.co.uk/content/news/hr-business-partner-models-fail-to-add-strategic-value-study-says

Writing in HR Magazine in March 2017, **Elizabeth Houldsworth**, course director of the **Henley Business School** MSc international human resource management programme said:

"In pursuing the business partner model HR has moved further away from some of the things it used to do well, for example the process and admin. When core processes such as <u>payroll administration</u> are not given sufficient emphasis the business loses reputation both internally and externally, and no amount of strategic business partnering is going to redress this."

This suggests that administration is the bedrock competency; I am sure that many payroll administrators would be shrugging their shoulders at the idea of HR knowing enough about payroll to be responsible for administering it.

In the same article, **Mark Swain**, Henley director of partnerships, opined:

"There isn't one best way, and we don't have a replacement in mind for Ulrich or similar. That said, in our report we talk about two ways that might work: 'evolve and transform'.

Evolve continues the general evolution of the HR function in applying its capabilities to a strategically significant role, combined with greater efficiency in delivery and expertise in matters relating to people. This essentially takes a set of capabilities and applies them to the organisation.

Transform is about HR responding to the future needs and context of business in the context of a defined purpose and outputs.

This essentially identifies a critical strategic organisational need and creates new entities to meet that need, building on the capabilities that the HR function has developed."

Charmi Patel, associate professor of international human resource management at Henley concluded:

"We don't necessarily need to consider a new business model. HR needs to stop being a cheerleader for initiatives it can neither enforce nor measure. Often I see HR leaders pleading with line or operational and financial managers to take on yet another set of 'people management' practices, burning up more social capital in the process. This is the very reason why talent development and people are not a clear priority for executive leadership. Evidence needs to be matched up and more than ever the HR profession now needs specialists in charge of bringing strategic thinking as a core HR in-house competence."

Source:
https://www.hrmagazine.co.uk/content/news/hr-business-partner-models-are-failing-so-what-next/

These commentaries from Henley go close to the heart of the HR mission: experienced specialists enabling the increase of capability within an organisation. If the HR business partner is the one doing it, great; it really doesn't matter what formal relationship HR professionals have with the business, the most important issue is that they are **INSIDE** the business, understand it, and have the strategic ability to be able to define ways to improve it via the workforce.

The crunch is really whether the ranks of HR people have that capacity for strategic thinking; thinking skills can be taught via self-improvement but it can take considerable time to manage such programmes, even were they included in mainstream HR professional studies.

The idea that by removing administration the function automatically becomes strategic is ingenuous, and any model, no matter how well-designed, is only going to work if the roles in that model are filled by people at the top of their game. Life usually doesn't work like that.

Chapter Three – Perceptions of HR

Both inside and outside of the profession everyone has a strong opinion about HR.

In October 2021, the **BBC** ran an article entitled *'Is HR ever really your friend?'* which was re-posted on **LinkedIn.** Here is a small sample of the typical comments there, all of which have been left unedited:

"When I started work the company had a Personnel Department who were approachable, helpful and engaging.

When I left work there was an HR department who were unapproachable, invisible, lacked empathy, did as the company hierarchy instructed and saw themselves as more important than the employees.

Clearly there to ensure the company stays the right side of legal in my opinion.

Just my view and experiences your HR department may be awesome"

"I remember when HR was there for me when my fiance lost her brother and brother in law in a car accident two weeks before Christmas.

Because I took more than a day off for her, I receisved a disciplinary.

Such a helpful department."

"In my experience, where HR appeared to have the employees' welfare at heart what they were really doing was making sure there would be no grounds for appeals, tribunals etc over grievances and dismissals."

"Speaking from experience - absolutely not! I would probably trust my worst enemy with my secrets before I trust HR."

"if you're being bullied at work..they side with the company in my experience and also seems to be the norm from what I've heard from my clients.. hence I now work for myself so I don't

have to put up with any corporate bullshit ever again"

"Where I worked they had no interest in employees whatsoever & made a right mess of the figures given to me for redundancy & pension amounts"

Really? I have NEVER thought of HR as being my friend. Some of the most unpleasant, incompetent and breathtakingly unfeeling people I have ever met worked in HR. And they were all untouchable."

"HR, protecting the Company from the workforce !!

Now back in the days of the BR Staff Office it worked a lot better as those who worked & were in charge had a better idea of how things worked."

"Based on my experience in NHS there was no support frm HR. I had to go into a disciplinary facing a panel of 14 including HR on my own. I was not in the union and was not allowed to take a friend in fort support

I use to work for the NHS and I found HR to be a total "waste of space". Incompetence personified. And no, none of them were ever my friend. No one ever liked them. They were the company's SS."

There were a few comments defending HR, or at least not as critical as some:

"The comments here mostly don't seem to fully understand the role of HR. HR is there to advise managers on how to deal with situations within the realms of employment law. It is not there to take any sides, nor is it HR's responsibility to make the decisions on a course of action, it is an advisory function. The decision regarding action ultimately lies with the management."

"As someone who works in HR, I disagree with all of the comments on this post. Yes we work for the Company, but we always have the employees best interests at heart and we are there to ensure processes are followed for fairness & consistency."

"I would generally agree but have to say, HR really came through *for me when I was falsely accused of sexual harassment by a coworker. They knew the accuser, knew his history of trying to get other coworkers fired, they knew there was no merit to his accusation. Never the less we had to have an embarrassing meeting between HR, us, his manager and my manager. But I was cleared in the end and and it didn't go in my record."*

"Yes, they can be. It's not necessarily about company culture it's about the individual personally. I have known both good and bad HR people in my working life. Ultimately their role is to protect the organisation from getting sued, but some will also behave like human beings with thoughts and feelings and empathy. Empathy is a key skill more than anything.

Personally I've never liked the title Human Resources. I don't see myself as a resource. I'm a person that has a life and thoughts and feelings. A lot of people I speak to wish it would go back to personnel."

Source:
https://www.bbc.com/worklife/article/20211022-is-hr-ever-really-your-friend

Harsh words overall, but these were the opinions of people who had experience of dealing with HR departments, so they cannot easily be ignored. Those comments capture some of the worst aspects of HR, both real and perceived.

From what we see in all the above it looks like HR needs to stand up and clarify its role to all in the organisation, and herein lies the problem: if that role has not been sufficiently explored with the directorate, so how can you be transparent to the workforce as a whole?

But – and it's a big But - HR managers almost certainly have experienced an inner fear that defining the role precisely could lead to a loss of clout and prestige in the company. To be brutally honest if a spotlight was trained on what goes on in some HR departments that could well be the result.

If the workforce, who are part of our internal customer base, have a generally poor opinion of the function, we are going to struggle to convince anyone higher up that we are giving value. That dream of a Boardroom seat may not happen any time soon.

Is HR trying to manage too much upwardly and forgetting to engage with those around them?

In August 2022 **Raidió Teilifís Éireann** ran an interesting opinion piece:

"HR departments are often criticised by employees, but do they really deserve this bad rep?"

Their assertion was that HR is *"often portrayed negatively…the bearers of bad news such as job losses and company closures. They make everyone do boring training on the latest policies and are the one department to whom we are all beholden for our next pay rise or promotion. Any sign of trouble and its 'someone will have to get on to HR'."*

We've already seen that this concept does not accord with what we have in mind as the true mission of HR.; the article continued:

"So where did HR go wrong?" and went on to say *"The essential problem is that this relationship between the employer and the employee is interdependent - two parties who both need something from the other. But like many relationships, it is dynamic and complex, influenced by factors such as diverse and conflicting needs. It also occurs in an environment where everyone is not necessarily equal, as the employer typically holds all the power. It is only when both parties are working towards the same goal that co-operation, motivation and productivity are achieved for the benefit of all, a mutual gain."*

"…Unfortunately, it is rarely the shareholders and leaders who lose out given the power relationship in organisations. Typically, it is the employee on the receiving end of poor HR practice. Employees who do not, for example, get to avail of new ways of working because HR have failed to ensure their shareholders and leaders understand the mutual gain inherent in flexible

working practices."

The suggested solutions were:

"…HR should be staffed with expert HR professionals who know what best practice looks like.

…these professionals need to be willing and able to shape shareholder and leader perspectives of the mutual gain in good HR practice – to hold them to account.

…HR needs to be properly resourced to work with all leaders and managers to ensure the HR practice is aligned with business strategy and implemented as the evidence-based design intended. This means HR need to be both strategic and present, regularly out on the shop floor, engaged with managers and employees on a regular basis and sufficiently resourced to allow this happen."

Their conclusion:

"If you are experiencing bad HR, then maybe it's because your organisation's shareholders and leaders do not value or believe in good HR. If you are a HR professional, go find an organisation with shareholders and leaders who do. And if you are an employee, ensure your interests are represented by a trade union"

Source:
https://www.rte.ie/brainstorm/2022/0209/1278696-human-resources-management-hr-departments-organisations/

'Best practice' is one of the most common expressions you will find in the world of HR, as if there existed a template Nirvana of procedural excellence to solve all ills.

'Best practice' as a concept is misleading because although there is an underpinning of compliance to every process and procedure, the operational aspects will vary from organisation to organisation, and like most procedures, becomes set in stone even when the world outside has moved on.

Anyone who belongs to any of the many online HR groups will see, almost daily, requests for template HR policies, and you just know those policies will be tweaked and fed into the new recipient handbook, even though they may not reflect the true values or workings of their organisation. I'm not a fan of 're-inventing the wheel' but I do think HR professionals should be capable of building their own policies that are both compliant and native to the employer.

A 2021 **Clear Review** performance report included these findings:

"An overwhelming number of HR leaders have negative views about people's performance whilst working from home."

"40% of HR leaders don't think that managers have the skills or training to have development and coaching conversations."

"Over 50% of managers don't the right tools to manage performance."

"Over 50% of HR leaders don't have the data to link performance and productivity"

Source:
https://www.clearreview.com/the-performance-management-report-2021-executive-summary/

The irony of this is that all these elements fall squarely within the HR remit, yet HR themselves are complaining that it's not happening.

During the March 2022 **P&O Ferries** debacle, an article in **HRZone** opined:

"P&O sackings remind HR to be the radical voice of the business" and urging HR *"to uphold their role as the people's champion"*

People's champion? Really? If that's how employers start to view HR, then it should be no surprise if the function gets side-lined as a result.

Furthermore, in the article:

"HR should be an outlier in a business. The days of being a mere service provider to the organisation are in the past. Our job today is to be a radical voice that stands for the values of the organisation, and a representative of the people who work in the business."

In the P&O Ferries case, HR truly **did** reflect the values of the organisation – and they were repugnant - but there is nothing behind this rallying cry to suggest how they should be representing the workforce. My guess is that if HR attempted to assume this radical mantle it would find itself outsourced in no time.

Again, in this same article:

"imagine the conversations around the HR table that could have led to such a course of action. What would we have done? Would we have spoken out or towed the line?"

Even the very fact that doubt exists on this question shows the extent to which certain people in HR have sold out their values and principles. How can the function profess to lead by example with such attitudes of cynical pragmatism? The article asks other questions which could be relevant; the point is that once again the role of HR was under the magnifying glass. In the P&O case it was found wanting, both in influence and moral fibre.

Source:
https://www.hrzone.com/lead/culture/po-sackings-remind-hr-to-be-the-radical-voice-of-the-business

In May 2022, **Unleash** published an article entitled **"Dear UNLEASH: Why won't leaders buy-in to HR?"**

One expert averred that *"Some executives simply may not understand the importance of an efficiently run and relevant HR function, while others may see it as a necessary expense for a non-revenue generating department. Either way, it is almost impossible to build a relationship with leadership teams that don't see the value of HR."*

Source:

https://www.unleash.ai/strategy-and-leadership/dear-unleash-why-wont-leaders-buy-in-to-hr/

My view is that if the C-suite don't see the value of HR, we should be asking why they employed the function in the first place, and what they think it should be doing. And it is at that point that the real conversation can begin.

We can't keep saying that the Board doesn't understand; we need to be specific about the mission and show the business reason for it.

The **Daily Telegraph** set out its HR stall in June 2022 with an article by **Juliet Samuel** (a columnist who covers politics, economics, foreign policy and technology) headed ***"How the HR monster destroyed the workplace"*** and sub-headed ***"Mission creep has turned the once humdrum human resources department into an ultra-woke, bureaucratic beast"***

The influential and highly respected HR professional **Ruth Cornish (Chartered FCIPD)** re-posted this article in **LinkedIn** and gave this commentary: (edited):

"We all know HR is a bad brand. You just need to go to a dinner party and say what you do & it won't be long before someone thinks they are hilarious and says 'human remains'. But equally none of us work in HR to make peoples' lives difficult. So what has gone wrong? If anything?

There is a huge difference between what an internal HR department does versus the growing number of Independents providing external HR services.

I wouldn't disagree that in many companies HR is the department that says No. Feared by many. Including the CEO which is ridiculous. But compliance with legislation and concern about employment tribunals is a big factor.

Yet many companies heavily relied on HR during the pandemic and if any of you got into trouble at work or wanted a big promotion & could phone a friend, it would be someone in HR.

Do you agree with this article and, if so, does internal HR need a makeover. My view is yes. I've seen HR done brilliantly and badly and everything in between. My view is that companies who get HR right, find it much easier to compete. Hire staff quickly. Promote without bureaucracy. Empowered managers that can get on with it."

Ruth Cornish identifies a major issue in that the function needs a makeover. I would add that part of that makeover needs to be a much clearer re-stating of what HR does, and for what it is responsible. Too many re-brands have been cosmetic with fancy titles and buzzwords, lacking in any in-depth reassessment of the actual function.

Source:
https://www.linkedin.com/posts/ruthcornish_how-the-hr-monster-destroyed-the-workplace-activity-6943810884649545728-fX78?utm_source=linkedin_share&utm_medium=member_desktop_web

Finally, in October 2022, In October 2022, **Darren A Smith**, a Forbes Business Council member posted an article in HR.com entitled '"**In The Words Of A Popular US Game Show, 'HR, You Are The Weakest Link – Goodbye"'**

This was reposted in LinkedIn where I commented on the following extracts:

"However, the big piece that front-line managers often miss is that, as managers of people, the HR department is the one that has the employees' best interests at heart."

Me: 'No, HR are not managers of people; the only people HR manage are HR people. Everyone else is managed by the line.'

Me: *"After all, engaged employees will do +20% more than they should"*

is a formula for burnout as far as I'm concerned and harks back to the pre-Pandemic era.

"HR is the advocate for all employees, and without considering people, companies achieve nothing. The people's voice is the one that HR represents."

Me: 'So what are worker's councils and unions for? Any HR pro who sets themselves up at the 'workers' champion' is asking for a quick exit.'

I summarised in another post on this thread:

Me: 'All of the various shades of opinion show how the whole concept of HR is fragmented and varies from person to person, organisation to organisation in a way that no other business activity such as Finance or Marketing is viewed.

The function has been ripe for overhaul for a number of years, but there are too many ingrained behaviours and vested interests for that to happen any time soon.'

The overall perception of HR is indifferent at best, and only by giving more clarity about the function are we going to start to change that.

Chapter Four – HR People

'Why do you want to work in HR?' is the question that is usually answered by *'Because I want to work with people.'* My response to this has always been *'Well you won't get much chance of that because you'll be dealing with management most of the time'.* Cue Exit, Stage Left.

HR people are the same as accountants, salespeople and product developers; the majority want to do a good job in the hope of a just reward and the satisfaction that achievement brings. Because of the people / workforce element, they have an opportunity to see the impact of their work if they do it right – or wrong.

At the end of 2020, **Sage** published a blog *"**Why I love working in HR: 14 HR experts explain why the love what they do and share tips for success."***

One of the main themes that run through many of the responses is the variety of the work, and that is certainly true of everything in the HR mission.

Source:
https://www.sage.com/en-gb/blog/hr-why-love-sector-career-tips/

According to the CIPD in September 2021, in the UK:

"78% of people professionals work in the private sector, compared with 21% in the public sector.

Overall, 60% of the profession is female and 40% is male. This split is still reflected in more senior roles (61% are female and 39% are male) but is much more pronounced in junior roles, where 91% of those in HR administrative roles are female, compared to just 9% of men.

91% of people professionals are white and 9% BAME. This compares to 88% in the workforce as a whole versus 12%."

Source:
https://www.cipd.co.uk/knowledge/strategy/hr/uk-people-profession-numbers#gref

In 2022, **Zippia** gave estimated statistics for the US, using a database of 30 million profiles:

"There are over 299,440 human resources managers currently employed in the United States.

70.3% of all human resources managers are women, while 29.7% are men.

The most common ethnicity of human resources managers is White (64.9%), followed by Hispanic or Latino (15.5%) and Black or African American (11.2%).

13% of all human resources managers are LGBT.

Human resources managers are more likely to work at public companies in comparison to private companies."

Source:
https://www.zippia.com/human-resources-manager-jobs/demographics

It's worth noting that there is a numerical preponderance of women in the profession overall, although not necessarily occupying the 'commanding heights' and that the ethnic band is far wider in the US.

Many people enter the profession by studying for professional HR qualifications – perhaps even going on to do a Masters – and then move into the world of work with little or no experience of how business works in practice.

Their first jobs will in all probability be as 'grunts' in an HR department doing not much more than administration, and they'll learn their HR 'craft' from HR people who have let this type of work flourish and expand. Plenty of daily 'firefighting' will keep them away from thinking too deeply about what they are doing, what they *should* be doing or even what the bigger picture might be.

'If only we could get rid of this admin stuff, we could be more strategic' is one HR mantra, but are we sure that all these HR people even have the capacity to be strategic? Can we turn an HR admin person into a business-focused powerhouse?

It's only in the past few decades that we have seen HR populated largely by people **whose only working experience has been in the HR function**.

It's no coincidence that some of the best HR professionals I've ever worked with originally came from a non-HR background, and some of those have moved on to the C-suite with notable success. They worked in the business and got to understand the nuts and bolts of it, and that's not something you can learn from textbooks or pushing paperwork.

HR needs to understand the business, talk the same language as the business, and not fall into the trap of thinking that it is a self-sufficient stand-alone activity.

Unfortunately, there is still a hard core of HR managers who believe they should command and control the workforce, and weak, lazy managements only too happy to abdicate the responsibility to them.

Finally, I want to touch on the subject of HR 'influencers'.

The whole of Western culture has developed an obsession with lists and ratings ranging from Best Hotels to Worst Sci-Fi films. HR is no exception, and every year there is a slew of awards and plaudits for those deemed most worthy by judges or HR peers.

Apart from renowned HR professionals and garlanded academics, the lists have also in the past featured HR heads who have presided over failed big businesses and large bodies that later were found to be hotbeds of corruption, cover-ups and racism. It seems that many of us are impressed by the job title and the size of the enterprise, rather than any ground-breaking initiatives in the world of HR.

Indeed, if you regularly scrutinise the lists of these 'influencers' you will notice the preponderance of HR heads who come from well-resourced bodies – sometimes publicly-funded, businesses and thinkers dispensing knowledge from the comparative safety of academia.

It occurs to me that a more appropriate set of heroes and heroines would come from the massed ranks of HR professionals who succeed in the task despite budget limitations and a constant battle against sections of the Boardroom. Perhaps some of these should be keynote speakers at the big conferences, rather than the Heads of businesses so large and almost monopolistic that their HR experiences couldn't possibly resonate with the audience.

Chapter Five – HR Organisations

The principal HR body in the UK is the **Chartered Institute of Personnel and Development (CIPD)** that has its beginnings in the early 20th Century.

It is published as having around 160,000 members and had a £2 million operating surplus in 2021.

The USA equivalent is the **Society for Human Resource Management (SHRM)**, founded in 1948, with around 285,000 members in 2022.

Both have come in for increasing criticism in recent years for their lack of progress in promoting or advancing the profession.

In June 2021, **Kathryn Jeacock** posted an open letter to the CEO of the **CIPD** (unedited):

"Dear Peter,

I'm writing to you as a passionate, people practitioner who has devoted the last 15 years to my profession within Human Resources and has diligently paid my membership subscription each year. I'll be frank, I'm getting fed up with the CIPD. I hate to break it to you, but I'm not the only one, so too are many other HR professionals.

*I felt compelled to write this open letter after reading an article in the latest edition of 'People Management' - **'The multibillion-dollar firm with no people team – why some businesses choose to forgo the function and what HR can do about it' (pp. 38 – 41)**. I rolled my eyes after reading the first few sentences when the article opened with 'what can the profession do to prove* its worth'....   Here we go again, this is where the fatigue and fed up'ness comes from. For the last 15 years CIPD has had the same rhetoric about HR proving its worth... it's getting really boring now. Something is clearly wrong with the profession if it's still suffering with this issue. We need to stop ignoring this fact and do something about it! We have stagnated. We need to start radically innovating... there is a whole movement of us starting to do this work already, with or without CIPD.

What annoyed me, was that a progressive, forward thinking, 21st Century Organisation (Octopus Energy), has taken an innovative approach around its people practices and how to best utilise people experts. Rather than taking the stance of 'what can we learn from it', the narrative was 'what can we do about it'. As a progressive and innovative People Practitioner myself, I want to continuously learn and evolve how I deploy people practices within organisations, this could have been a great learning moment. Instead, the article was peppered with a bland and moaning narrative that focussed on addressing the issue as a PR problem and how HR needs to promote itself better, share more success stories and talk about how excellent we are. It remained somewhat silent on the question raised about why people have had a less than positive experience of the profession.

I'll be bold and say as a profession we are not excellent. Yes, there are many talented and wonderful people who work within HR, but we are bound and constricted by outdated employment legislation and policies that frankly seek to protect against litigation rather than problem solve, resolve conflict, and drive performance. Most HR people know that grievances procedures don't resolve problems and disciplinary's are not a 'learning experience' (see ACAS). The CIPD should be lobbying for change in legislation that maintains the protection of people in work but is more humane and person-centred. As a starter for ten, why are we still calling ourselves 'Human Resources'? How outdated is this terminology! Same as CIPD still referencing 'Personnel' in its name! I know changing what we call ourselves is the tip of the iceberg, but language is important, it's how we make sense of the world.

I implore the CIPD to stop whingeing and get on and evolve the profession. As mentioned, there is a growing movement within the People Practitioner community calling for change and doing this already. CIPD needs to become part of this movement or risk alienating large swathes of the community. As organisations increasingly change their ways of working, to meet the 21st Century needs of the technology and knowledge economy, People Specialists and the likes of CIPD need to be leading the way on this stuff.

For the first time in 15 years, I've debated whether to renew my CIPD membership. I'm not alone in this consideration either. I'm disenchanted and fed up. I'm holding out one last hope that CIPD still take the reins and lead the forefront of this exciting movement (I'll be honest though, I'm not convinced).

To all the People Practitioners out there who crave change and a better way of looking after people in organisations, to those who are open to adapting and evolving in our roles as People Specialists - keep up the good work! Progress is slow but change is coming and COVID has accelerated the scale and pace of change. We need to get uncomfortable, for in the discomfort is where we will evolve and grow – we can't be protectionist or ignorant anymore, it's time to innovate.

Yours sincerely

Kathryn"

One respondent commented:

"I've been banging on about this for years. I'm sick of our profession being denigrated by the very institution that we pay to promote it. (CEO) seems to have only one aim and that's to increase the coffers by expanding the membership. Little innovation or forward thinking behind articles or the promotion or motivation of its members."

Source:
https://www.linkedin.com/pulse/last-week-i-sent-letter-ceo-cipd-kathryn-jeacock/

This certainly echoes criticism I hear regularly in HR circles both in-person and online. There is the impression that CIPD has a captive membership, as those that quit and stop paying automatically lose the letters for which they studied so hard. Imagine how that would play in the world of university degrees!

The earlier perception of 'no letters – no HR job' that once represented good business for CIPD has now well and truly been put to rest.

In November 2022, **Kelly Swingler** wrote this post in **LinkedIn** just after the 2022 CIPD Annual Conference and Exhibition (ACE). Addressed to the CEO of the **CIPD**, it opened yet another avenue of dissatisfaction with the way things are (unedited):

…*"#CIPDACE you disappoint me again and I am so tired and frustrated from having to moan about the same thing.*

Forbes have reported that 98% of HR Professionals are experiencing burnout, 98%! And from what I can see of your CIPDACE agenda you›ve run one session that includes the word burnout, and that›s a session on self-care.

Self-care does not fix burnout and it will not prevent it. When I burned out in 2013 I contacted you to ask for help, I was told to contact my EAP provider.

When I realised I was the fourth HRD in my company to become seriously ill as a result of Burnout I contacted you again, I was told to contact my EAP provider. My replacement died, and still no progress from you.

Since 2014 I have coached numerous burned out HR Pros, five of my clients currently are currently off work sick, as a result of burnout, all HR Pros. And you think it's enough to run one session on self-care and think you've done enough for the profession!! You are letting HR down, big time!

I no longer work in HR, my choice, but you were part of the reason for that. I love the HR profession, and I know the true value that HR adds. I also know the crap they have to deal with. And you have to do more to support them.

You MUST do better!!"

Kelly Swingler is a major loss to the mainstream profession, and her commentary is extremely relevant. The post drew many comments from fellow professionals:

"Woo! HR can be a really frustrating profession and so can be the CIPD but we are only human. I respect your honesty in this post. So sorry about the burnout you faced.

I agree ACE looked disappointing."

"Absolutely!"

"I sacked my membership off 5 years ago and haven't missed it! I actually feel a better HR professional for having sod all to do with them quite honestly. You only have to look at the number of HR vacancies there are to see just how many people are leaving the profession."

"They need new blood and a big shake up with leaders that actually give a shit about the people in HR instead of more HR policy.

We've spoken about this SO much, and it really upsets me to see just how little they do." **Kelly Swingler**

"CIPD will never change. As I was told by them "more and more people are signing up each year." What they need is some competition to make them buck up their ideas... something we are more than capable of doing" in reply to Kelly's last remark.

"*I am no longer a member of CIPD for so many reasons, mainly that they are so out of touch with the real world. I am part of the -- community which offers much more sound advice but also, we also have well-being champions, mental health champions, and lots of great forward-thinking support!*

Until hashtag #CIPD makes radical changes I will not be a returning member."

A few months later, Carolyn Hobdey, a consultant, educator and author turned up the heat. Under the strapline **"I think the CIPD needs a re-brand"**, she wrote a **LinkedIn** article which included a telling paragraph:

"*To me, it feels like the CIPD has teeth but no bite. They have become commentators on, not shapers of, change which is how being an HR Director within an organisation frequently feels. We feel the need to ask what they think, then immediately want to NOT do what they recommend. This isn't satisfying for anyone.*"

Across the Atlantic, this is what star HR disruptor / commentator **Laurie Ruettimann** had to say on **SHRM**:

"SHRM...What Did You Do?

When it comes to SHRM, we HR people all have a "more love than hate relationship" with the organization.

A hashtag that says #FixItSHRM was recently created, referring to a recent tweet released by SHRM featuring a graphic focused on improving DEI at work. Unfortunately, the photo used severely lacks diversity. To make matters worse, this incident happened right at the start of Black History Month.

This incident isn't the first time, either. Similar issues with the organization were brought up in the past. However, the most recent tweet still holds a certain shock level for many people— including Joey, "It did surprise me that it's 2022, of all the things we've gone through in the past few years about diversity and the reasons why diversity is on the forefront for a lot of minds and a lot of employers, for the largest body of HR to get it wrong, that was surprising."

Lars shared a similar sentiment. While he doesn't hate SHRM, he is "incredibly disappointed by them."

DEI has been at the forefront for many companies. With the rise of social injustice and discrimination in the workforce, people want to see organizations genuinely put in the effort to change. "For the field of HR who has been through so much in the last two and a half years to have a "governing body" that just doesn't seem to put in the effort, is just incredibly disappointing," Lars shares.

It all boils down to relevance. Unfortunately, SHRM has not shown they are up-to-date with modern HR teams and functions. Because of this, Lars believes that "they've lost a whole generation of operators that they'll never get back," disappointing HR professionals working to create actual change.

Getting Criticism on Criticism

SHRM has half a million member HR professionals in its ranks and is profitable for the first time in years. They are hitting all of the benchmarks for success. So when they see criticism online, their first thought is to criticize that criticism. But that approach begs the question, "Is all of this is necessary?"

More and more organizations are stepping up to become a venue where HR professionals can connect, share, and grow in the ways they want and need. SHRM is no longer the only resource available to HR professionals. "SHRM might say that a tree is falling in Twitter and is not making a sound, but the industry is saying otherwise. And I think the topics that are being covered in places like Lars, what you're covering and your cohorts, and Laurie, what you're doing on your show, are topics that we aren't seeing SHRM cover. We're not seeing analytics, AI, agile HR. We're not seeing those sorts of things that are really what business leaders are looking for from HR," Joey says.

The world of HR is changing, and SHRM's tweeting incident seems to suggest that the organization isn't in tune with the macro conversations currently happening in the HR space. "The world of work is changing, and HR has an opportunity to directly shape and influence what this looks like," Lars explains. "We're building kind of a new post-industrial revolution era of work, and we're still getting articles on SHRM about dress code. Yes, that might be petty of me to kind of call them out on that, but I remember that came out in Q4. It was just like, how out of touch are you talking about tattoos at work?"

While many voices in the Twitter-verse tweet out different sentiments of criticism, there is truth to what they are saying. "We may be voices in Twitter, and they may say what they'll say, but I think we're onto something, and where there's smoke, there's fire. And again, we all love SHRM. So we want to see it win. It's an institution. It's not just the people in it; it stands for something. It means something. Just want to see it relevant in the years to come," Joey says.

What Can Be Learned

SHRM has an opportunity to learn and grow, but that can't happen without first changing the dialogue and putting diverse voices within the organization.

"I don't think they've got the right voices steering where they're going. I think that again, there's a huge population, particularly on the leading modern, progressive wing of HR, that has nothing to do with SHRM. And so even if they were speaking to SHRM, SHRM's certainly not listening to them," Lars shares.

While putting new voices into the organization will help drive change, listening to what others are saying can create a modern future for the organization. "SHRM prides itself on being the voice of HR. And I think right now, it should be the ears of HR. Listening to what folks on Twitter are saying, what industry is saying about HR," Joey says.

SHRM's efforts to listen to what people are saying means connecting with them without just brushing off the criticism. "It would really be reaching out to some of those leaders who are on the cutting edge, bring them in for round tables, maybe evaluate board positions and content ideas and see what can be *done to guide the conversation as opposed to being reactionary to it," Joey says."*

Source:
https://laurieruettimann.com/what-is-with-shrm-joey-price-lars-schmidt/

Conclusion

It seems that the established institutions are falling out of step with the needs and advanced thinking of their membership. The very same bodies that once used the Disruption word are themselves being disrupted both from within and without – and either not liking it or doing nothing about it. They are talking about adjusting to what is referred to as the New Normal – in other words rebuilding the establishment. My take on this is there won't be any New Normal any time soon.

Right now, real thought leadership is coming from groups on the periphery and radical individuals like **Laurie Ruettiman, Kelly Swingler,** (both having moved from the profession mainstream), **Ruth Cornish, Siobhan McHale** and **Jason Averbrook**, among many others, advocating newer technologies and a human approach, all helping to shine a searchlight on HR's true path forward in the world of work and business. I should also mention here the sterling underpinning work done by **The Maturity**

Institute and Council Member **Paul Kearns** whose analytical approach to both organisations and HR merits much wider recognition.

MISSION: HR
PART TWO – A NEW WAY

Summary – The Real Mission

Experience has shown me that the core mission of HR almost certainly lies in getting and putting into use the right tools to enable good management and employee development for better performance.

These tools, for example, would include HR systems to generate management data, a pay and benefits structure to reward the workforce and Recruitment and Development programmes to max employee potential, and so on.

All this needs to be underpinned by a framework of compliance both with statutory requirements and organisational aspirations such as Equal Opportunities for all, further reinforced with communication and the necessary learning for management figures and employees alike as to their responsibilities within their roles.

HR doesn't have to be a nest of legal eagles, but they do need to know the working basics of Employment Law – enough to cope initially with most issues – and where and when to get specialised advice. And remember, if the full programme is rolled out, you'll have fewer cases arising from trigger-happy managers and disgruntled employees.

What I've said here sounds straightforward, but it won't be music to the ears of those whose principal aspiration is an HR seat at the Board table and the trappings that that entails. It's not a glamorous role I'm suggesting, and it won't grab too many headlines - but it's a crucial one, and if it's done right, it makes the difference between a well-run organisation and one that is running at somewhat less than its true potential.

Furthermore, getting all this to work as a well-integrated plan will indicate that the HR professional has a true grasp of the strategic thinking necessary to be successful, irrespective of fancy job titles.

Chapter Six – Technology

HR has been reluctant in the past to get involved too closely with Technology, allowing either Information Technology, Finance or even external consultancies make the decisions on their behalf (which, of course is a great disclaimer when things don't work out as anticipated), or they've gone ahead in a scattergun way and selected software that is totally unsuitable.

A while back I posited **Three Laws of HR tech***, which in essence placed firmly in HR's domain the responsibilities for selecting and installing the HR system, maintaining its data integrity, and ensuring that the information in it was available freely to those who need it.

Let's be brutally honest; it's not just yesterday that HR and managements woke up to the fact that we need information. It started in earnest in the late '90s, when savvy managements and HR managers started using data from their PC-based HR systems for decision making. Modern software with automation, self-service and simpler report writers makes it even easier to access to that information.

The **First Law** states that *"HR will take responsibility to ensure that their organisation has an HR system configurable to meet its process and information needs."*

It would be fair to say that managements have been flying blind for a long time. I've seen the turmoil when an urgent request for employee information is handed down to HR. Panic. The inaccurate and outdated data in the HR system is exported into a spreadsheet, and then hours of tweaking and manipulation follow, as unprocessed leavers, starters and changes are changed around. The report that eventually ends up with management is still strewn with inaccuracies at the end of it all.

From this arises the **Second Law**: *"HR will be responsible for the accuracy and timeliness of information held in the system, providing a single source of truth and real-time reporting."*

HR's task is to maintain the HR data both current and accurate, and that is not as easy as it would seem. Throughout my consulting career, I've yet to meet a client who could swear, hand on heart, that their data was completely trustworthy. If it's 99% accurate it's as good as useless.

With the first two Laws functioning well, it's necessary to understand that HR's role is not to act as gatekeepers for the data. The data is business data and needs to be available to all those authorised to use it.

Even now, a client HR director or manager will say to me "Great! Now we'll be able to give them those reports when they ask for them." Wrong. Those internal requests will disappear, because those needing reports will access them directly from the system whenever they need them.

Hence the **Third Law: *"HR system information will be freely available and in required formats to all in the organisation authorised to have access to this information."***

Part of the blame for the all the disorder described above can be laid at the door of those same managements who insisted that Information Technology folk drove the selection process, on the basis that HR were not qualified to make these decisions. Well, looking back over the years at all the systems that IT selected, it seems IT weren't too darned smart either, and their selection criteria completely discounted the user experience; sexy architecture, the ability to sit on their existing obsolescent hardware and compatibility with other outdated in-house systems were the key criteria.

Some of the problem also stemmed from HR being over-optimistic about what was to be delivered and expecting vendors to configure the software with the minimum of input and time resource that they could bother to provide. And, occasionally, to make things worse, when the system didn't work as intended, they abandoned it and sourced a new one without correcting the methodology.

Technology now gets simpler and more intuitive, and the need for data has driven its own learning process. HR are now acutely aware of the needs of management and are suggesting enhancements where previously they hadn't been specified.

My Three Laws aren't disruptive, but I think it's time that the responsibilities were formally accepted. *If* HR has abdicated its role in ensuring that a functioning system is in place, *if* the data in the system is decidedly unreliable and *if* HR is still acting as a gatekeeper for management information, then it's time to change – and change *now* before change is imposed on HR. How we go about this is covered in Chapter Twenty.

Chapter Seven – Management Information

In November 2022, **ExpertHR** published a .pdf document titled *'Key workforce metrics for business success'* available for download

They cited the following measures, and went on to describe why they were important:

"Labour turnover

Cost and time per hire

Absence

Employment engagement

Diversity"

Source:
xperthr.co.uk

These are typical headings for metrics or statistics that can be pulled out of the HR system. Reports from the HR system are of interest to everyone in the organisation, so as well as being the key source of information, it is also a showcase for HR and its capabilities, meaning that data must be accurate and as close to real-time as is possible.

Every organisation will have its own reporting requirements, and the format and data need to be agreed with the directorate and each business unit, so that the templates can be set up and merged into your reporting suite.

In July 2021, **Sage** gave insights into the management information management the C-suite wanted from the HR department, probably because they were mostly based on data held in the HR system (unedited):

"What HR data does the c-suite want? When we asked business execs what information they would find most valuable for informing their decision making we saw overwhelming demand for the following metrics"

"These were the top 15 metrics that business leaders said they want from HR:

Headcount – 94% of c-suite execs said they wanted this

Employee productivity rate – 94% of c-suite execs said they wanted this

Cost per hire (93%)

HR to FTE ratio (93%)

Training rates (93%)

Employee satisfaction (93%)

Revenue per FTE (91%)

Turnover rates (91%)

Labor cost per FTE (91%)

Cost per employee (91%)

Promotion rate (91%)

Average tenure (91%)

Diversity percentage (91%)

New hire failure rate (90%)

External time to fill (90%)"

Source:
https://www.sage.com/en-gb/news/press-releases/2021/07/
c-suite-execs-reveal-the-top-hr-metrics-they-need/

Firstly, note that these are not metrics for the HR department but are figures for the overall workforce. Some of these are not metrics but plain statistics and in practice many of them are wrongly applied as measures for HR performance, which we will be looking at in Chapter Ten.

I see reporting as falling into four main types:

a. Management & Compliance

b. Operational

c. Costs and

d. Organisation.

These inevitably have some overlap. Here are some examples:

a. Management & Compliance

Headcount and Salary

Generally, a full time employee working 35 hrs / week will be counted as 1.0 Full-Time Equivalent (FTE) . Therefore, a part time employee working 17.5 hrs / week will be counted as 0.5 FTE.

Gender Pay Gap and other pay gaps

"The unadjusted gender pay gap is defined as the difference between the average gross hourly earnings of men and women expressed as a percentage of the average gross hourly earnings of men. It is calculated for enterprises with 10 or more employees"

Source:
https://ec.europa.eu/eurostat/statistics-explained/index.
php?title=Gender_pay_gap_statistics#:~:text=The%20
unadjusted%20gender%20pay%20gap%20is%20defined%20
as%20the%20difference,with%2010%20or%20more%20
employees.

This same principle should be applied to other groups such as Ethnic, Disability and Age.

Minimum Wage confirmation

In 2017, Nearly 700 firms were fined total of £1.4m for not paying minimum wage (*Guardian - 6 January 2017*) and nearly 200 firms were 'named and shamed' for minimum wage underpayment. (*People Management 5 August 2021*)

There is absolutely no excuse for this, as all the information needed to comply is held in the HR system.

Employee Relations (Discipline, Grievance & Appeal)

Numbers of each and outcomes analysed by manager and business unit

Succession

Common succession planning metrics include:

Dividing the number of employees from the succession plan promoted by the number of employees promoted to a vacant role.

Critical Positions Filled Internally and Management Positions Filled Internally. These two measures obviously go together. And if you have the data, look for ways to incorporate costs into the scorecard.

b. Operational

Absence Rate

Absence rate in any period is calculated by the number of sick days absence divided by the annual number of working days available and multiplying by 100. Example:

Department A

Annual total sickness absence days = 49

Annual working days available = 250

Absence rate is 49 divided by 250 x 100 = 19.6%

Learning & Development activity

To arrive at the effectiveness of Learning & Development you need to look at all employees who have undertaken L & D activity in a given period which should include at least 3-6 months after that activity. There should be a marked improvement in performance providing:

-The training was in response to a skills gap identified at a previous review and

-The training was effective.

You will need to develop measures for the various activities, including actual production or milestones reached to arrive at the improvement figure, and then relate back the total spent on development to see if it gave value.

One commonly used measure of Return on Investment (ROI) is:

Value of Performance Improvement (PI) – Cost of development training

Divided by Cost of training and multiplied by 100 to give the percentage ROI. Example:

Training course costs 1000

Employee annual salary is 30,000

Performance Improvement (PI) = 5%

Value of PI = 5% of 30,000 = 1500

Value of PI – Cost of training x 100

----

divided by Cost of training

$$\frac{1500\text{-}1000 \times 100}{100} = \text{50,000 divided by 1000} = \text{ROI of 50\%}$$

Overall Retention rate

Retention rate is the percentage of employees who remain at a company for a fixed time period. To calculate this, divide the number of employees who stayed during a specific time period by the number of employees at the start of the time period and then multiply by 100. Example:

On January 1st there were 120 employees

On December 31st 88 of those employees were still with the company.

Therefore 88 / 120 x 100 = 73.33% Retention Rate.

This can be analysed out between business units, departments or even grade levels for comparison.

Performance

By business unit or individual within that business unit, actual progress measure against agreed milestones.

Recruitment

Cost per hire:

Amount spent on recruitment + amount / time resource spent on training before fully effective ÷ number of new hires

Acceptance percentage rate: (Number of people who reject a job offer ÷ number of offers made) x100

Effectiveness percentage of recruitment sources: (Number of successful applicants from a source ÷ total number of applicants from a source) x100

Service and Staff statistics

Average Length of Service: (Total years' service ÷ number of employees)

Example:

10 employees have a combined total of 48 years.

Average Length of Service is 48 ÷10 = 4.8 years

Average staff levels can be calculated by by adding the start and finish   workforce and dividing by two

Example:

Number of employees 1st January = 196

Number of employees 31st December = 204

Average staff number is 196+204=400 divided by 2 = 200

Workforce

Workforce turnover is calculated by dividing the number of employees who leave in a year (or other specified period) by the average number of employees at the organization during the same period.

Voluntary turnover as a percentage of all employee turnover. In that case, you would divide the number of employees who left voluntarily by the number of all employees who have left in a specified period.

Involuntary turnover is measured using the same method.

c. Costs

Average Benefit Cost Per Employee:

This is calculated by taking the total costs of benefits and dividing by the number of employees. However, it is best to analyse by grade or level of employee to avoid skewing the average, and by department for insight into distribution of costs across the business.

Revenue per employee:

Total sales revenue ÷ Number of employees

Measuring revenue per employee gives you a measure of the output of your employees on a more granular level and can help you measure your employees' productivity. It can also help you compare your spending and your profit.

The staff cost ratio formula is a way of presenting the cost of labour in a business as a percentage of revenue. To work out the staff cost ratio, you use the following formula: (Total cost of labour over the period ÷ Gross revenue generated over the period) x 100

Overtime: Number of hours worked overtime per year, per employee

Calculating the extra time your staff are spending in the office can be helpful to see where the need for extra resources and manpower lies. It can also help you identify areas where productivity might be falling short.

d. Organisational

Organisation chart

Bias detection *(see below)*

Diversity Equity & Inclusion (DEI) analysis

The most common way is through demographics such as gender, race, age, and ethnicity disability/medical.

These are physical and are apparent.

Invisible diversity refers to the characteristics that are not readily apparent such as disability, religion, sexual orientation, military experience, socioeconomic background, marital status, national origin, and more.

A June 2020 a **Personio** survey of the HR pandemic situation

showed that 48% of respondents lack the data and tools needed to support the business in the best way possible, and 71% have struggled with poor access to employee data.

> Source:
> https://www.personio.com/blog/half-of-hr-managers-say-hr-needs-to-change-post-pandemic-as-strategic-planning-proves-vital-to-success/

This is a tough indictment of HR's inability to grab the benefits on offer in terms of improved quality of output from their HR systems.

A later article in 2023 published in **HR Magazine** showed that things aren't changing too quickly. Entitled **"HR struggling to get grip on data amid workforce challenges"** it commented on a report by the **CIPD** ' *Effective workforce reporting: Improving people data for business leaders'*

> *It found that "HR and business leaders said their top areas of concern were skills and labour shortages, inflation costs, wages and wage inflation, and employee health and wellbeing.*
>
> *Yet just under half (46%) of organisations collected data on recruitment and retention, and just 33% said it was regularly reviewed.*

It was a similar picture for diversity data, where 46% collected data, yet only 24% reviewed it.

Similar ratios were also reported for employee wellbeing data organisations and training and development."

Tim Grimes, co-founder of flexible jobs platform WorkYourWay commented that "HR's failure to use data meant it was making decisions in the dark. If organisations continue to turn a blind eye to the reasons behind a lack of diversity and inclusion, or if companies just throw more resources at hiring instead of spending time understanding retention and labour shortages, they'll be having the same issues year in and year out, with no end in sight or tangible improvement."

He may be off track with the notion that HR make decisions based on the data, but they should certainly make the data available to management, and give recommendations based on it. So are management not taking an interest in the data, or do they have little faith in it? Remember in our technology section we emphasise the importance of accurate and timely data; a few errors can cause total lack of credibility.

In the same article, **Katie Jacobs, CIPD senior stakeholder lead**, said HR professionals can sometimes fall into the trap of creating an industry around data.

"Businesses and HR teams sometimes collect people data for the sake of it, presenting it without context and not considering how it connects to business priorities.

HR professionals need to be systems thinkers, thinking holistically about what the information is telling them, how it links to organisational objectives and outcomes, and what actionable insights can be gained from reporting on and reviewing it."

That is a fair assessment of the role that HR should be playing with data, but data and insights have only so much value. If it is not being seen and actioned by those with executive powers, then the risks of ignoring it should be spelled out in clear terms.

Source:
https://www.hrmagazine.co.uk/content/news/hr-struggling-to-get-grip-on-data-amid-workforce-challenges

HR (People) Analytics

The **Gartner Glossary** defines this as "...the collection and application of talent data to improve critical talent and business outcomes. HR analytics leaders enable HR leaders to develop data-driven insights to inform talent decisions, improve workforce processes and promote positive employee experience."

Source:
https://www.gartner.com/en/human-resources/glossary/hr-analytics

In 2015 **Josh Bersin** wrote in **Forbes**:

"The Geeks Arrive In HR: People Analytics Is Here"

"The old fashioned fuddy-duddy HR department is changing. The Geeks have arrived.

Today, for the first time in the fifteen years I've been an analyst, human resources departments are getting serious about analytics. And I mean serious.

I was in a meeting several weeks ago in San Francisco and we had eight PhD statisticians, engineers, and computer scientists together, all working on people analytics for their companies. These are serious mathematicians and data scientists trying to apply data science to the people side of their businesses.

This last week I had another similar meeting and we had three of the world's leading insurance companies, two large retailers, three health care companies, and two manufacturing companies with serious mathematicians and scientists assigned to HR.

As I recently discussed in the article "**How People Management is Replacing Talent Management**?" there is a major shift taking *place in the market for people analytics. After years of talking about the opportunity to apply data to people decisions, companies are now stepping up and making the investment. And more exciting than that, the serious math and data people are flocking to HR."*

Source:
https://www.forbes.com/sites/joshbersin/2015/02/01/geeks-arrive-in-hr-people-analytics-is-here/

I once asked an HR journalist to explain why an organisation he was reporting on had three Harvard graduates analysing data in the HR dept instead of releasing it to line managers to analyse and he responded:

"Most of them don't have the skills or time to take care of that. In theory that makes sense, but in practice it would ruin the data to focus exclusively on people analytics"

Make of that what you will. My contention is that we need to keep the analytics question simple and digestible. HR professionals themselves should be given a grounding in the science to ensure the function's self-sufficiency, otherwise you finish up with people in the department who nobody knows what they are doing, in the same way that IT dominated HR systems in the early days.

The most practical way of delivering analytics to the business is by setting up accessible dashboards in the HR system that reflect the various measures that need to be monitored. The integrity of the data must be 100% accurate, or else everyone is wasting their time, and it goes without saying that all the data fields needed for the analytics must be present and populated, and that this data should be in one place – the HR system – to form the essential 'single source of truth'.

These dashboards either come as integral to the HR reporting module or can be built by hooking a business intelligence tool* *(see Appendix)* into the HR database and extracting the required information to present in a visual format.

A favourite analytic for businesses is **labour turnover** or **attrition**, although there is more than one viewpoint on this. With high turnover you have an expensive way to operate, but is low turnover always a good thing?

Turnover analysis reveals more when broken into levels or grades; people will leave from lower levels if their progression pathway is blocked in the middle and upper levels, and these are the very people it is cost effective to develop. As a result, it is necessary to have gradual churn in the management layers to free up opportunities as well as admit 'new blood' and new ideas.

Time to hire is another measure and indicates how an employer is shaping up in the job market. If time to hire is unduly long, it could mean that either the reward package is not competitive enough or the organisation has a doubtful reputation. If time to hire is short, then careers with the employer would seem attractive to candidates, although the figures could be skewed if the organisation is a major employer in a district, and therefore 'the only game in town'.

Bias

An inescapable fact of modern business life is that of bias in the workforce, both in recruitment and in the actual career trajectory in employment. Bias based on gender, orientation, ethnicity, age, and health is to be found everywhere, in many cases unconsciously. Background can also come into play where some employers show a clear preference for Oxbridge or Ivy League graduates for their recruiting intake.

Most organisations actively want to eliminate bias but are uncertain how to start, and this is where technology can provide the answer by demonstrating the status quo based on existing personnel records. Reports can be built to track the career and benefits trajectory of each group inside the organisation, and if that organisation is truly committed to equality, then steps will be taken to correct the imbalances.

This can't be achieved in five minutes, but a plan of how this can be achieved in the shortest possible time should be drawn up, approved, and rolled out.

Human Resource Accounting

Despite the title, the reporting from this methodology more properly belongs in the Management Information category, as the results are affected by a wide range of policies and actions within the organisation.

One definition of HRA would be that expressed by **Accounting Tools**:

"Human resource accounting involves the tracking of all costs related to employees in a separate report. These costs include employee compensation, payroll taxes, benefits, training, and recruiting. Such an accounting system can be used to determine where human resources costs are especially heavy or light in an organization.

This information can be used to redirect employees toward those activities to which they can bring the most value. Conversely, the report can be used to identify those areas in which employee costs are too high, which may lead to a reduction in force or a reallocation of staff away from those areas."

You will notice that this definition incorporates some of the elements we have identified for our management reporting.

The definition goes on to say:

"Rather than looking at employees as costs, the system is redirected toward viewing them as assets. This can involve the assignment of values to employees based on their experience, education, innovativeness, leadership, and so forth. This can be a difficult area in which to achieve a verifiable level of quantification, and so may have limited value from a management perspective.

From an accounting perspective, the expense-based view of human resources is quite easy - employee costs from the various departments are simply aggregated into a report. The employee valuation approach is not a tenable concept for the accountant, since this is an internally-generated intangible asset, and so cannot be recorded in the accounting system."

Source:
https://www.accountingtools.com/articles/human-resource-accounting.html

I am sure that many of my fellow HR professionals would instinctively argue against the rigid application of this concept. It is true to say that of late the tendency **has** been to treat employee as assets, especially when those assets become expendable for a variety of motives.

Whatever measures and methodologies we use, information is only of value if it is accurate, timely, relevant, and made available to the right people at the right time. The decisions and actions that follow on from this information are all-important.

Chapter Eight – Compliance

Fundamental to every organisation are the policies and procedures which determine the way in which work is done, behaviour in the workplace and_steps that need to be taken by either or both sides in the event of certain things happening – or not happening.

Some of these reflect statutory obligations, others will relate only to the individual organisation, although none of the latter can run counter to legal requirements.

What is important is that they are all accessible right across the organisation, either in contract or handbook form or online through an intranet or other portal. Equally important is that the obligatory policies are in place on the dates they become law. In corporate life I rarely saw policies come out in time and this is not at all acceptable.

If necessary, briefing sessions and training workshops can be held to highlight any topics of particular importance or interest, or even online videos with quiz to test understanding.

There should be **no employee or manager who is not fully aware of their rights and obligations** in carrying out their duties and being able to comply with them.

Some major causes of employment conflicts can be:

Management inconsistency or unequal treatment

Harassment and / or bullying

Communication failures

Lack of clarity in a job role or task to be performed

Insufficient training

Issues with the workplace itself.

Lack of opportunity

Personality clashes

and I'm sure most HR professionals will have encountered these at some stage of their career.

Everyone should be clear as to how they can get recourse for any situation, without it prejudicing their jobs. This is done by having a clear-cut route to raise grievances or complaints, and a robust procedure to obtain the facts for examination by persons not directly affected by the issues.

Central to this is that management themselves must follow those same procedures and not seek to short-circuit them by 'paying people off' or ignoring the problem in the hope that it resolves itself. To be aware of a problem and do nothing about it will make the employer just as liable as if they were responsible for it.

HR can facilitate compliance by producing easily understood policies and procedures, using workshop sessions if necessary. One only needs to look at the number of employment problems that go legal to appreciate how important it is that everyone is clear on what should happen.

In my professional career I've seen tribunal cases go against both employers and employees for the simple reason that they didn't follow the laid-down procedures correctly or in a timely way. Managers sometimes tend to act in a 'knee-jerk way', and employees either voice their complaints to the wrong people or wait too long to express them.

Key policies you should have, and that all employees must know (in alphabetical order):

Absence

Data Privacy

Employee Relations – Disciplinary, Dismissal, Grievance & Appeal

Employer Code of Conduct – e.g. Punctuality, Attendance, Behaviour

Health & Safety

Learning & Development

Non-Discrimination / Equality & Diversity

Pay & Benefits

Performance management

Probation

Termination

HR procedures will, of course, vary according from organisation to organisation, but they must combine both the legal obligations of both employer and employee with specific terms set by the organisation, none of which can conflict with current employment legislation.

Remember, any policy that is not present or clear will default to the legal position, which could be open to interpretation – and therefore potentially costly – so take time to make sure you have everything in place, and that everyone is aware; they should at least confirm that they have read through, and sign for it.

Chapter Nine – Employee Wellness

The universal realisation that employees need to be looked after had dawned some years before the COVID-19 pandemic, but the most common solution at that time was to contract an Employee Assistance Programme (EAP).

The **Chron** newsletter gave this definition:

"Employee assistance programs, also called EAPs, are employer-funded programs designed to provide a variety of services to employees in need. EAPs are usually staffed by licensed professionals, including clinical social workers, mental health counsellors and substance abuse professionals (SAPs). While the pros of an EAP often appear to outweigh the cons, the truth is that the benefits or detriments are largely dependent on the employer, staff and work environment."

Source:
https://work.chron.com/pros-cons-employee-assistance-program-12009.html

The cost was typically calculated on an agreed range of services offered across the board by providers at a per capita per annum subscription and was the most convenient way for employers to access solutions for the multiple situations that arise with employees.

The pandemic led to a more detailed focus on the effectiveness of EAPs. In February 2022, **Yulife** published a blog entitled ***"EAP is not a last resort: The evolution of EAPs in a post-pandemic world"*** which concluded:

"While there are some aspects of EAPs that are yet to catch up with its rapid change, the EAP industry has still got some big changes on the horizon. The pandemic has been the catalyst for unprecedented change in the world of work, and Galliano predicts that this will progress even further still."

Source:
https://yulife.com/blog/eap-is-not-a-last-resort-the-evolution-of-eaps-in-a-post-pandemic-world/

It is quite possible that the expansion of scope and depth in EAP services will reflect in the price. Awareness among employers and employees has been accelerated by the pandemic and raised workforce wellness to priority status.

Forbes reported in February 2022 that:

"employers…moving to a fully remote workforce significantly improved their business. Employer surveying by the management consulting firm McKinsey & Company has found that productivity, engagement, and morale on the job skyrocketed during the pandemic. Fifty-two percent of employers report their employees are more engaged. Only 19% say engagement has declined.

Yet, paradoxically, mental health concerns and burnout have skyrocketed. Nearly six times as many employers report increased mental health issues among employees since the pandemic began—burnout being among the most common. "

Source:
https://www.forbes.com/sites/forbesbooksauthors/2022/02/01/mental-health-in-a-post-pandemic-world/?sh=1fa991663b7a

Burnout is the new workforce nemesis, as typified by this article in **The HR Directo**r magazine in early 2022 headlined:

"Burnout is causing three-quarters of UK (white-collar) workers to consider quitting"

Source:
https://www.thehrdirector.com/business-news/employee-engagement/three-quarters-of-uk-workers-considering-quitting-their-jobs-due-to-burnout/

According to the **Global Wellness Institute**

'in February 2020, only five percent of all working hours in the US were done at home. By May 2020, this number skyrocketed to 60 percent. Now, as we head into 2022, that number is holding steady at around 40 percent.

Working long hours can take a toll on your mental and physical health. It can even lead to premature death. A study from the World Health Organization (WHO) found that a shocking 750,000 people die due to long working hours every year (considered working 55 or more hours per week).'

Source:
https://press.fourseasons.com/westlakevillage/trending-now/workplace-wellness/

An unfortunate outcome of pandemic and subsequent remote or hybrid working is that people occupy their erstwhile commuting time with work, and without proper oversight this can easily lead to exhaustion and burnout. A simple way to control excessive working is to restrict access to business systems to the contracted hours and allowing this to be overridden by logged access requests. This won't be popular with businesses who have grown rich on the unpaid efforts of their workforce ('employee loyalty'), but it is becoming a necessity in the face of what has disparagingly been called **'quiet quitting'** i.e., working the hours one is paid for by employees who have realised that there is a Life beyond work. This has more correctly been called **'the great reset'.**

Employers owe a duty of care to their workforces, failure to do so being an increasingly expensive exercise, and so need to protect their employees as well as look to reduce their liability risk. Technology and better- trained management can make work a fairer and more fulfilling activity giving better results for the organisation.

HR technology is used to gather data and insights, but new technology is already available to monitor employees on a regular basis for stress points and refer for human intervention.

Apart from deteriorating mental states caused by emergency

working conditions and poor management, the pandemic may have spawned an increase in workplace harassment. Certainly, **Fast Company** felt as much and reported in 2021 that:

"One of the surprising consequences of working from home during the pandemic is that employees reported an increase in workplace harassment." and went on to describe some typical scenarios.

They also stated that in a *"recent Project Include survey, 25% of respondents said they experienced an increase in gender-based harassment during the pandemic, 10% said the same of hostility related to their race or ethnicity, and 23% of those 50 years and older reported a jump in age-related abuse."*

Source:
https://www.fastcompany.com/90655155/why-workplace-harassment-increased-during-the-pandemic

In 2017, the **BBC** surveyed 2,000 respondents and showed *"that most victims of sexual harassment didn't report the violation. Either in fear of retaliation or if the harassment was played off as a joke, more than half of all victims stayed silent. "*

Another survey showed that *"75% of sexual harassment cases in the workplace are unreported. This statistic shows that organizations need to do a better job in cultivating a culture to show that it's encouraged to file sexual harassment complaints. "*

Source:

https://inspiredelearning.com/blog/sexual-harassment-in-the-workplace-statistics/

In December 2020, **Payfit** led with :

"Employee wellbeing – HR's #1 priority"

"The number one challenge for HR professionals in 2020 was employee wellbeing with 37% reporting that it was most common within their department.

For several years now, organisations have been aware of the impact of employee wellbeing on company performance and finances. This was reflected in our data, with 50% of the HR professionals we surveyed revealing that employee wellbeing had the most significant impact on company success.

However, organisations have found that the policies and programmes put in place before the pandemic were incompatible with remote work. This has led some to realise that there is much more to employee wellbeing than they had initially conceived. Consequently, many have looked to evolve their programmes to meet four critical criteria:

- *physical.*
- *mental.*
- *financial.*
- *recognition."*

Source:
https://switch.payfit.com/en/hr-trends-pre-post-pandemic-employee-wellbeing/

These are important steps for safety at work, not only for mental health, but also for physical as well. Just handing off the problems to an Employee Assistance Programme provider may not be sufficient in these times to look after the employee and reduce the risk of employer liability.

Chapter Ten – Measuring HR

I was once told that HR needed to justify its existence in the company. My reply was that if the Board didn't know why they had HR, why did they continue to employ them?

There's plenty of confusion about HR metrics; all too often they get muddled up with management workforce metrics, or worse, are just figures without meaning or correlation.

Ways must be found to measure the effectiveness of the function, or we have no way of knowing if it is succeeding or failing.

In a May 25th 2022 webinar session, **Sage** reported on '**the top ten most used HR metrics by People leaders today'.** In order, with percentages, they were:

'Candidates interviewed by hirer *41%*

HR to full-time employees ratio *41%*

Labour cost per full-time employee.......*40%*

Headcount...*40%*

Vacation days taken...............................*39%*

Cost per hire..*37%*

Turnover rates (in- & voluntary).............*36%*

Cost per employee.................................*35%*

Absenteeism rate *35%*

Training rates...*34%'*

Apart from the fact that the data are in the HR system, I contend that HR has very little direct input to these, as senior and line management have this very much in their purview.

Number of candidates interviewed by hirer is irrelevant as there is no comparator with hire success.

'HR to full-time employees' ratio. There is no reference point for this other than to benchmark other similar organisations, but even that is rendered doubtful by the fact that there may be unknown radical differences under the surface.

Cost per hire is determined by the nature of the job and the means used to fill it and does not particularly reflect any measure of HR effectiveness.

Training rates, along with **Total Training days** and **Total Training spend** year on year are just numbers that give no sense of value and **Vacation Days** taken is also just a number in isolation.

Absenteeism, unless properly focused, is more a question for the business units concerned, as are the **Turnover** rates.

Headcount, **Cost per Employee** and **Labour Cost per Employee** are figures more related to organisational policy and operational considerations.

All in all, irrespective of their real significance, these would more properly be referred to as Workforce Statistics and not HR Metrics. It is apparent, however, that the People leaders polled had little idea of what the figures they were using actually signified.

In April 2022, **Personnel Today** featured *"**Two-thirds of Employers do not collect enough HR performance data"***

"Absence management data (86.8%), staff turnover data (84.7%), exit interview feedback (83.9%) and results of staff surveys (79.8%), emerged as the most commonly captured measurements by HR teams.

However, the three least commonly collected HR performance data categories were "time to fill vacancies data" (36%), "cost per hire" (32.2%), and "time to competence data" (9.1%), information that is fundamental to an effective recruitment and retention.

The research also found that 60% of organisations do not compare their HR performance data to other organisations."

Source:
https://www.personneltoday.com/hr/hr-performance-
data-2022/?ID=zzrzf~9nzjhn~qhrhz~W4ik~Ky0gk&
utm_campaign=email&utm_medium=email&utm_
source=newsletter&utm_content=

We've already seen that these are mainly workforce statistics. The issue about benchmarking this workforce information can be looked at in various ways; my personal view is that unless you are in direct competition with those you are benchmarking against and that competition is a zero sum game, it's hard to see what real benefit is to be gained.

Another statistic that has a popular following is **Engagement rating**

In 1990, a psychologist from Boston University, **William Kahn**, propounded three dimensions of employee engagement:

"Physical engagement

Relating to the extent to which employees expend their efforts, both physical and mental, as they go about their jobs. Kahn used examples of employees describing themselves as 'flying around' during their work and experiencing high levels of personal engagement during that time. He linked the ability to expend physical and mental energy at work with increased feelings of confidence.

Cognitive engagement

To be engaged at this level, employees need to know what their employer's vision and strategies are, and what performance they need to deliver to contribute to them as much as possible. Kahn also drew attention to the meaning that people attached to their work, theorising that more knowledge encouraged more creativity and confident decision making.

Emotional engagement

This is based upon the emotional relationship that employees feel with their employer. A positive relationship will require the organisation to learn how to create a sense of belonging at work, encouraging employees to trust and buy in to the values and mission of the company. Kahn cited the likes of positive interpersonal relations, group dynamics and management styles as practices that would make people feel safe and trusted."

There is a widely held view that 'engaged' is equal to 'happy' but in fact people can be quite happy being non-productive, wasting time at work, not being stretched by their daily activities, and drawing a comfortable salary, which any truly engaged employee would not be content to do.

Source:
Psychological Conditions of Personal Engagement and Disengagement (Academy of Management Journal, December 1990, Vol. 3, no. 4, pp 692-724)

Also:
https://journals.aom.org/doi/abs/10.5465/256287
https://www.talkfreely.com/blog/dimensions-of-employee-engagement

Effectiveness of HR software

Harking back to my **Three Laws of HR Tech**:

"HR will take responsibility to ensure that their organisation has an HR system configurable to meet its process and information needs."

"HR will be responsible for the accuracy and timeliness of information held in the system, providing a single source of truth and real-time reporting."

"HR system information will be freely available and in required formats to all in the organisation authorised to have access to this information."

If you are meeting these three to the satisfaction of your internal clients all the way up to the Board, you are winning!

Add to that the ongoing return on investment on the current HR software application; you'll find that on your original application for funds to acquire the system. Check if it's still 'the gift that keeps on giving' – or if it ever gave in the first place.

Measuring the value of HR has always been a tricky business. At first, it was said by HR that 'you can't really measure what we do' a view that was dismantled when **Drucker's 'you can't manage what you can't measure'** became widely accepted

Here I suggest some more ideas on metrics we could apply to HR itself, with regards to value and effectiveness.

1. **The amount of legal advice fees incurred by the HR department**

If you have experienced and qualified HR professionals working for you, these charges should be minimal, as they won't – or shouldn't - be consulting expensive lawyers every time a problem arises. If, on the other hand, you entrust HR to the calibre of administrators and people who organise the Christmas party, then your savings on salaries will be more than outweighed by legal bills – or tribunal awards.

Following on from this:

2. **Number of tribunal cases fought and won / lost**

This is a great indicator of whether your line manager training is taking root, as most cases will arise from this area.

3. **Number of tribunal cases paid to 'go away'**

4. The number of dismissals dressed up to look like Redundancies with a pay-out value above the prescribed norm.

5. **The number of compromise agreements / NDAs (Non-Disclosure Agreements) drawn up to cover up management failures.**

Numbers 2-5 demonstrate the organisation's belief in its policies, and the ability of its senior officers to adhere to them. If you are paying lots of employees to make your troubles go away, then your organisation is not following its own policies and procedures. An objective appraisal of what is happening is a matter of extreme urgency.

Number 5 is indicative of a toxic culture. The practice of compromise agreements will spread like wildfire through an organisation if unchecked; I have seen companies where they issue these for every single leaving employee. Of course, it's expensive, as there is a legal implication for every one that is signed. HR's urgent task is to ensure the appropriate training for all in the front line. Failure to do this or continuing failure to comply will prove increasingly expensive.

6. Amounts unnecessarily paid out for 4 and 5

This will put a figure on all the failures of management in the matter of employee relations and HR's ability to enable compliance in these matters.

7. How many years that senior HR staff have been in post

This may be a generalisation – and I can guarantee will be controversial - but surely there is a limit to the amount of time needed to analyse the HR issues facing any organisation and put measures in place to solve them?

As with any other senior employee in your management structure, you need to be sure that they are continuing to be effective and not merely orbiting effortlessly, fielding the same problems year in, year out in what is called the "**resting and vesting**" syndrome.

8. Percentage of identified individual development needs that have been fulfilled within the specified period.

This should reflect procedures put in place by HR, executed by line management and monitored automatically by the HR system. The ongoing development of the workforce where necessary is a business priority for any organisation. The figure should be 100% or very close.

All these measures I have described are almost never in general view, but they do have a direct line of sight to how the HR department is performing.

It isn't just about HR, of course, it is principally a reflection on the organisational culture, starting from the very top. If senior managements are not prepared to make an investment in quality practitioners with properly identified roles, then they will pay for it indirectly, and if they already have those practitioners who are not pulling their weight, it's time to get managing them.

HR's constant quest to justify their existence has reached new levels of intensity as various academics and other much-lauded 'influencers' scratch around for metrics that will prove the value of HR, and that quest is ongoing.

MISSION: HR
PART THREE – HOT TOPICS

Summary

In this section, I look at some issues that confront HR or are in HR territory (which is not always the case!) and offer up some discussion or viewpoints that relate to them, together with my own comments.

It's true to say that most of these items have been hot for quite a while – decades, in fact, and they are recurrent themes at conferences, conclaves of HR folk, the press and online media.

Chapter Eleven – Culture

There's so much talk about organisational culture right now, not least because some employers insist that remote working will destroy the culture, while remote work supporters claim that this isn't so.

The important points are who creates the culture and is it possible to change it.

The **Harvard Business Review** in its article in February 2021 stated that *"Company Culture Is Everyone's Responsibility"*

Source:
https://hbr.org/2021/02/company-culture-is-everyones-responsibility#:~:text=In%20a%20new%20culture%2Dbuilding,organizations%20actually%20operate%20these%20days.

This view is very much the modern consensus, although consciously or otherwise, the C-suite is the exemplar; if it is failing at that level, then there isn't much chance for the rest.

Earlier, (2018) **HR Future** had placed the job squarely on the HR function:

"…More accurately, the person who is responsible for the company's culture is the HR Director, HR Executive, Head of HR, HR Lead or any other title you wish to give the senior HR Professional in the company.

If you're a senior HR Professional, compare what your company claims to be its culture with the behaviour of its employees. If there's a gap between the two, you've got a lot of work to do. Senior HR Professionals who refuse to take responsibility for their company's culture should be held accountable. They are responsible for the people, so they are responsible for the way people behave in the company."

Which of course runs completely counter to what the HR mission should be about. Culture is like Quality Control – it should be a part of every employee's work ethic and not handed off to some department as an impossible task to manage, and an easy target to blame. Added to which, of course, HR are **not** responsible for the people, as we have already seen.

Source:
https://www.hrfuture.net/talent-management/personal-development/who-s-responsible-for-your-company-s-culture/

I don't propose to add much to what has already been said, but let's imagine that we were looking for a series of statements describing the culture we would like in our own enterprise; here are some very simplistic yet effective examples:

'I want people to be able to give of their best at work'

'I want the working environment to be conducive to good performance'

'Everyone should have the equipment and skills to do their job'

'I'd like all employees to have the opportunity to realise their potential'

'I'd like employees to be proud to work for this company'

'My employees should always feel comfortable enough to share any concerns they may have with their manager or appropriate company officer.'

'I have procedures in place that ensure that any grievance is investigated and acted upon to achieve a resolution.'

'No employee will receive unduly more favourable treatment over another employee'

'Every employee will participate in the success of the company.'

It's not really that difficult, is it? And I'm not saying that work should be 'fun' and that everyone must be 'happy'. It's about getting things done, and having the right people properly equipped and with a willing mindset to do them.

Chapter Twelve –Diversity, Equity & Inclusion (DEI)

Diversity, equity, and inclusion (DEI) is a term used to describe policies and programmes that promote the active participation of different groups of individuals, including people of different ages, races and ethnicities, abilities and disabilities, genders, religions, backgrounds, cultures, and sexual orientations.

The advancement of these initiatives more often falls to HR, although without solid backing and resource from the Board, they are almost certain to fail.

Let's begin by saying that we know that it's the right thing to do from a societal standpoint. However, when we start to look at the business side, things aren't quite so clear-cut.

There are any number of studies and articles in circulation that

demonstrate that DEI can improve business performance such as in May 2022:

'....**McKinsey** research shows that over a several-year timeframe, racially diverse companies are 35% more likely to outperform their less diverse counterparts, while from a gender standpoint, companies with strong women representation are 25% more likely to outperform.'

Source:
https://www.marketsmedia.com/diverse-firms-outperform-research-shows/#:~:text=According%20
to%20Robinson%2C%20McKinsey%20research,25%25%20
more%20likely%20to%20outperform.

Note that this is from a gender-only standpoint, and here we start to see the complexities of the issue.

In June 2022, **Kim Elsesser** a leading gender equality advocate, writing in **Forbes** reported that:

'(in the US) Business spending on diversity, equity and inclusion (DEI) initiatives has skyrocketed in the last decade. It's estimated the global market for DEI reached $7.5 billion in 2020 and is expected to double by 2026. To justify these initiatives, many organizations claim a diverse workforce is good for business'

She went on to say that:

'....experts are cautioning that using this business case to justify diversity initiatives may backfire.

New research reveals that linking diversity to corporate profits may be a turnoff for the underrepresented individuals the organizations are trying to attract. In fact, the use of the business case to justify diversity can result in underrepresented groups anticipating less belonging to organizations, which, in turn, makes them ultimately less likely to want to join the organization.'

Source:
https://www.forbes.com/sites/kimelsesser/2022/06/20/the-business-case-for-diversity-is-backfiring/?sh=1f58a4b2351d

The same month, **Harvard Business Review** concurred:

'Eighty percent of Fortune 500 companies explain their interest in diversity by making some form of a business case: justifying diversity in the workplace on the grounds that it benefits companies' bottom line. And yet, in a recent study, the authors found that this approach actually makes underrepresented job candidates a lot less interested in working with an organization.

This is because rhetoric that makes the business case for diversity sends a subtle yet impactful signal that organizations view employees from underrepresented groups as a means to an end, ultimately undermining DEI efforts before employers have even had the chance to interact with potential employees.

Based on their findings, the authors suggest that if organizations must justify their commitment to diversity, they should do so by making a fairness case — that is, an argument based in moral grounds — but to achieve the best results, they should consider not making any case at all.

After all, companies don't feel the need to explain why they believe in values such as innovation, resilience, or integrity. So why treat diversity any differently?

Source:
https://hbr.org/2022/06/stop-making-the-business-case-for-diversity

The root of the problem is that there is no cast-iron business case with numbers showing a direct line of sight between DEI and business performance, and even if there were, which strand/s of the DEI elements would that relate to? Because DEI not only relates to physical aspects, but also to unseen ones, at which point we need to consider Neuro diversity.

An invaluable description of Neuro diversity is that given by **Texthelp:**

*'...the term used to describe **natural variations in the human brain**. It relates to differences in the way we think, process, learn and behave. Most people are neurotypical meaning that the brain functions and processes in the way that society expects. 1 in 5 people are neurodivergent meaning their brain functions differently in one or more ways than is considered standard or typical. Their unique traits are often characterized as ‹neurodiverse conditions›.*

Source:
https://www.texthelp.com/resources/neurodiversity/

So, DEI isn't necessarily visible, although that is the criterion most applied by business because it is most easily addressed, leading to the phenomenon that blows a hole through the best efforts of any initiative to bring about Change: Corporate Tokenism, viz, in April 2022:

'Since 2017, the number of FTSE 100 companies with someone from an ethnic minority background on the board has doubled, from 47% to 94%. In terms of directorship, this has also doubled, from 8% to 16% directors. The FTSE 250 has also seen an increase to 55% of companies with someone from an ethnic minority on their board. However, progress is slower and more needs to happen on FTSE250 boards. The target is for every FTSE 250 company to have at least one person from an ethnic minority on the board.'

Source:
https://better-boards.com/the-status-of-ethnic-diversity-on-ftse-boards/

Well-intentioned, no doubt, but barely scratching at the surface of the DEI issue. What about Gender and the other DEI strands, not to mention Neuro diversity?

In a **LinkedIn** post, October 17th 2022, **Safia Boot**, **Director of Respect at Work Ltd**, stated:

"The representation route is an easy way to say 'oh look we have one of them, so we are not racist' _Representation without inclusion in decision making is mere Tokenism which some BAME will accept as vanity appointments only to later wise up they are temporary useful fools aka likes of Suella Braverman et Al. Therein lies Institutional Racism as it begs to ask the question 'how did we get to this situation historically and what social practices and policies are we enacting daily to reinforce the homogeneity?'

#HRSoWhite is part of the barrier and hence explains the glacial change. CIPD only woke up to its part in failing to prioritise antiracism onto its agenda until 23 June 2021 post George Floyd and then failed to roll out to branch level or address the numerous

ET cases that reference HR failings in race discrimination cases which are only the tip of the iceberg as vast numbers never get to this stage.'

Source:
LinkedIn

A much lauded but misleading example of DEI was the composition of the Conservative government under Boris Johnson and its succeeding administrations; here there were women and ethnic minorities very much to the fore, but true diversity was absent **because their thinking was all very much of the same order coming from the Right wing of the Conservative Party**.

Given all these considerations, what can HR do as part of the mission?

The very first step must be to review the people that you have. You will already have the physical attributes in your workforce database, so there needs to be an audit for neuro diversity, and if 20% of people are neuro divergent, this category must not be ignored.

At first attempt I would advise that this is best left to experts in this field, such as ***https://exceptionalindividuals.com***

Alternatively, individuals can take online tests to check whether they have neuro diversity traits, and with their collaboration, work to ensure that their workplace needs are taken into consideration.

After that, you should overhaul your recruitment practices, to give a level playing field to all candidates who can do the job.

Hire Ventures set out an excellent guide on how to do this with particular focus on recruiting diverse candidates and creating a diverse workforce and this is worth repeating:

'…diversity refers to the makeup of your company. It's looking at the differences between us and acknowledging how they make us unique. These differences can come in visible and invisible forms.

Visible diversity refers to the characteristics that can be readily seen such as age, sex, or race.

These differences are easier to identify, process, and define, but there is much more to an individual than their physical appearance! This is where invisible diversity comes into play!

Invisible diversity refers to the characteristics that cannot be readily seen such as disability, religion, sexual orientation, military experience, socioeconomic background, marital status, nation origin, and more.

Invisible diversity encapsulates our backgrounds, experiences, and characteristics that make us truly unique individuals.'

They list six essential tips to help ensure that your recruiting process is inclusive and values both visible and invisible diversities:

1. Don't assume everyone is like you, even if they look like you

'...shared physical characteristics don't equal shared life experiences. There are different demographic invisible diversities like religion, sexual orientation, gender identity, and education level that impact the way we live and experience society. There are also psychological invisible diversities like values, beliefs, attitudes, personality, cognitive and behavioural styles, as well as knowledge, skills, and abilities. All these factors make us all different people and individuals.'

2. Don't expect disclosure

'A 2011 study found that 88% of people with invisible disabilities have a negative view of disclosing their disability. While many people with disabilities ask for accommodations in the workplace, some don't want to reveal their disability. This does not apply to just disabilities but also any form of invisible diversity.

Many people are "passing" and able to hide their invisible social identities. They might fabricate, conceal, or use discretion to hide because of fear of discrimination or harassment.'

'.. We can't expect everyone to share the deepest parts of their identity. All we can do as leaders in our organizations is to create a safe environment where people will feel comfortable sharing if they want to.

If employees do disclose their invisible diversity, believe them. You shouldn't ask them to prove it. Many people with disabilities do not fit what a stereotypical person with a disability may look like.'

'...If someone comes to HR to ask for an accommodation, regardless of how surprised you may be, follow your regular process, acquire medical documentation if necessary, and don't push the topic any further. Questioning a person's disability can cause them additional pain, shame, and to feel unwelcome in your organization.'

3. Be aware of social cues

'Many times, when people are uncomfortable, they might not immediately tell you about one of their invisible diversities. This discomfort may be out of fear of repercussions, so the person may use social cues as a way to feel out their environment and to start subtly disclosing their identity. For example, if someone is trying to conceal their sexual orientation at work and someone repeatedly asks them about who they are dating, they might try to send signs that they are uncomfortable. This can be by sending messages, dropping hints, or giving clues. Sometimes people want to see how their colleagues will react before completely disclosing their invisible diversity.

The best thing we can do is to reduce saying things that might be misconstrued as offensive even if you did not have malicious intent. Also, try to pick up on social cues when our colleagues might be uncomfortable or offended. If they are, apologize and avoid repeating the same mistake.'

4. Be inclusive with your language

Inclusive language is a way to neutralize language and not

make cultural assumptions. It's a great tool to help make your workplace more equitable. Practicing inclusive language means avoiding gendered words/phrases like "Hey guys" or "Ladies and Gentlemen." These phrases, while they probably didn't have negative intent, can negatively impact others. Using masculine phrases like "hey guys" can be a sign of unconscious bias. By opting to use gender-neutral phrases like "everybody," you can prevent accidentally misgendering a colleague.

5. Recognize that communication styles vary

People's communication styles are different! Not everyone talks the same way. People with different cultures might have different speech patterns and nonverbal communication styles. Neurodiverse people often have different communication styles and might not be able to easily verbalize what they are thinking. Life experiences often shape the way we communicate. It's important to respect how others communicate and try to be understanding and patient.

6. Advocate for education and awareness

One of the best recommendations for all types of diversity is to advocate for increased education and building awareness…'

'… By continuing to educate and learn more about invisible diversities, you can develop a team culture that not only spans the differences but celebrates them.'

Source:
https://hireventures.com/2021/07/22/visible-vs-invisible-diversity/

7. For those both managing and recruiting, I whole-heartedly support the '6 Behavioral Nudges to Reduce Bias in Hiring and Promotions' propounded by the authoritative Paola Cecchi-Dimeglio, a co-chair of the Executive Leadership Research Initiative for Women & Minority Attorneys at Harvard Law School and founder of the decision-making consulting firm

People Culture Drive Consulting Group.

"Summary

In today's talent marketplace, everybody is looking for new ways to make the best hiring and promotion decisions..."

"Everyone who has worked to get diversity right knows there is no elixir that increases diverse talent in leadership roles. Doing DEI by the numbers just won't get you there. But here's some good news: By focusing on <u>decision intelligence</u>, and on evidence-based solutions that drive scalable change and increase inclusion, leaders can increase the number of diverse candidates that they hire and promote."

"As an academic, I've long studied the problem of increasing employee diversity in companies, and as a consultant I've applied what I've learned to help companies hire and promote more fairly. Through this work, I've identified six behavioral nudges that together form an effective, well-rounded approach — one that can help executives make better, less-biased decisions in hiring and <u>promotion</u>."

1) Generate ranked criteria for candidates.

"Recruitment can be overwhelming for both interviewers and candidates. When overwhelmed, people tend to favor the familiar. But a strategic approach can help bring order to the process. According to <u>decision research</u>, having a solid list of pre-determined, prioritized qualifications for a position is key to choosing wisely. The hiring committee should agree on five to 10 qualifications, which may span both technical skills and business acumen, and rank them by importance..."

"Creating clear, succinct lists of qualifications provides a set of focal points that can steer decision-makers away from race, gender, and socioeconomic background. This strategy should generate diverse sets of options and can be used with a broad range of position types.

2) Challenge yourself to support the opposite opinion.

"An HR professional at a global professional services firm I worked with noticed that 89% of new hires were the first candidates seen. The committee wanted to counter this biasing tendency, so decision-makers applied a "thinking of the opposite" strategy."

3) Modify the environment.

"Different environments can improve or support high-quality decision-making and can impact organizations' hiring efforts. Seemingly small factors such as time slots, room arrangements, and a room's temperature can all exert influence on the decision-making process."

4) Invert the default rules.

Default rules may support or improve individual and social welfare. However, these unquestioned shortcuts often lock in bias. When attempting to increase the number of women or minorities hired into leadership roles, defaults can get in the way.

One midsize technology company that I worked with was stunned to learn that this was happening to them. When we assessed their promotion patterns, they expected to find patterns favorable to women and minorities, but we found the opposite. The company was routinely promoting the same groups.

5) Use planning prompts.

6) Shape information effectively.

"The right information isn't always enough. It has to arrive in a compelling format. To guide decisions and motivate people, communicators can frame some messages as gains and others as losses.

A persuasive message is only as good as its likelihood to trigger action. Reframing the message enables a broader range of recipients to respond. With an increase of applicants opting in, the pharma company built a stream of better prepared candidates."

There are case examples quoted for 5 & 6

Conclusion

"In today's talent marketplace, everybody is looking for new ways to make the best hiring and promotion decisions. The adaptable interventions I've laid out in this article build on proven best practices that foster good decision intelligence. As a leader you need to pay better attention to what you're getting, examine the data to determine why you're getting it, and make interventions that change the default thinking. Only then will you be able to hire, develop, and keep the talent"

Source:
https://hbr.org/2022/11/6-behavioral-nudges-to-reduce-bias-in-hiring-and-promotions

What we are seeing in the above initiatives is Humanity in action; a genuine desire to do right by both the people and the business. If we truly value our workforce, as most enterprises like to think they do, then making the effort will repay dividends, as our talent pool will be greatly increased by drawing in groups of individuals who formerly were not considered because they didn't 'fit in' with the existing culture for whatever reason.

Additionally, we must regularly ask our employees for feedback on what additional support they may need to perform better as situations can change.

Flexibility is another important aspect for many employees who have family or domestic responsibilities or perhaps an impediment to easily getting around.

All these initiatives will depend heavily on building trust in the workplace, always showing transparency and giving people the confidence to speak out about issues which are troubling them. This is not achieved overnight, but it is important to start right and give commitment to the ambition to make the workplace a good place to be, wherever that happens to be.

Chapter Thirteen – New Working Patterns

Despite many workers embracing the work-from-home model, in a City A.M. article in April 2021 headed '***Remote working is just as effective, but it can hurt pay and promotion, HR execs warn'***, **Sarah Loates**, founder of **Loates HR Consultancy** warned in **City A.M**. that *"remote working can affect people's promotion and earnings chances."*

"We have seen a definite increase in job candidates asking if the position they are applying for will allow for some working from home [but] people who work from home more are less likely to receive bonuses and may be hindering their chances of promotion,"

Source:
https://www.cityam.com/exclusive-home-working-is-just-as-effective-but-it-may-hurt-pay-and-promotion-hr-execs-warn/

Her observations are underpinned by a study by the Office of National Statistics (ONS) released in April 2021 which found that people who mainly worked from home prior to the pandemic were far less likely to have received a promotion or a bonus compared with their office-based counterparts.

Between 2011 and 2017, for example, those who usually worked from home were less than half as likely to have received a promotion compared with workers who consistently worked mainly away from home.

In terms of bonuses, those who mainly worked from home were

around 38 per cent less likely on average to have received a bonus compared with those who never worked from home between 2013 and 2020.

Source:
https://www.cityam.com/homeworkers-less-likely-to-be-promoted-or-get-bonus-then-office-counterparts/

Therefore, Loates warned that *"an often-overlooked downside of a hybrid approach is the potential for a '2-tier system of employment' to emerge."*

Source:
https://www.cityam.com/exclusive-home-working-is-just-as-effective-but-it-may-hurt-pay-and-promotion-hr-execs-warn/

I'm going to overlook the obvious discriminatory flavour of this whole question, as there must be policies in place and acted upon to stamp that out along with any other forms of discrimination. Ignore that, and you are in deep trouble.

But what becomes increasingly obvious is that as we find ourselves in times of great uncertainty, HR needs some tools not just to navigate through, but to try to ensure as much continuity as is possible.

Depending on your organisation, Employment contracts for office or field staff will no longer be one-size-fits-all. There are endless permutations on the remote / office theme and, providing they meet the needs of the business, all are perfectly OK.

On a remote work contract, an employee can undertake to be available say from 8.00 am to 6.00 pm Monday-Friday, take some agreed hours out during the day for chores and still cover the weekly hours required.

To keep track of these varying contracts, you're going to need a workforce software module that enables them to monitor their hours, not for control but for employee well-being.

When home working was forced on many people, they stopped

travelling and started to work ridiculous hours – because they could. Some people I know burned out in a matter of weeks because no-one was watching the situation. This is not sustainable – you owe a duty of care to those who work for you.

As an employer you need to ensure that your people don't stay too long at the screen without taking a break.

Additionally, consider closing access to some business systems outside of contracted hours unless entry is authorised and logged.

For these types of cases, system messages to this effect can be built in.

Of course, this won't play well with some bosses, but just imagine the cost of a claim for mental breakdown because a few common-sense safeguards weren't put in place.

If some of your people are going to work remotely, you must invest back some of the potential savings into giving them the tools to do the job, such as a good internet connection - with bandwidth to manage large files in some cases – computer, mobile device and – if you want to do it right – have their potential work area and furniture checked out. No point having your employees signed off with chronic back problem due to bad ergonomics.

And, if you are the employer you want to be – have the employee checked out. No matter how keen they are to work away from the office, they may not be psychologically equipped to perform optimally on their own and may need extra support. There are special enterprises who provide psychometric and ergonomic assessments for both employee and remote workplace.

Make sure your managers are upskilled to handle these new working patterns; the success of these initiatives will be in large part down to them.

It's all about making sure bases are covered for employee well-being, performance, and managing potential risk liability.

Chapter Fourteen – Outsourcing HR

There comes a time in the life of most CEOs and CFOs, when the question of outsourcing HR becomes a siren song. At one stroke, all those pesky workforce problems could be passed to some outside agency.

CFOs are the greatest champions of this idea because they've never been able to fully understand how HR is measured and so it's just a large business expense.

The professional services firm **Milestone** outlined some pros and cons in their September 2021 blog, and I have selected some salient ones:

"Advantages of human resource outsourcing

Cost

Perhaps the most attractive advantage of HR outsourcing involves cost reduction. By outsourcing certain functions, such as payroll or recruitment, organizations do not need to spend money hiring and training internal employees for those particular roles. Hiring an outsourced HR firm on a flat rate to contract is almost always less expensive than hiring an internal team.

Efficiency

Outsourcing HR functions gives business owners the ability to allocate time and resources to other endeavours. Outsourcing frees the business owners and company employees from having to work through HR processes, manage compliance, and recruit and exit employees. Once outsourced, the organization can take the time and money otherwise spent on these functions and redirect it to new projects, allowing it to stay competitive and speed up productivity.

Skills and Knowledge

An HR outsourcing firm will have fully-trained experts with in-depth knowledge and experience in how to handle even complex employee relations situations. An understanding of employment laws and regulations, even those that update frequently, such as taxes, safety requirements, payroll, and healthcare. HR specialists will stay up to date on the changes, understand more about legal compliance, and ensure the company is in compliance. In-house personnel who aren't trained in HR may not have as good an understanding of the law and regulations that are subject to change and struggle to keep the company up to date and compliant."

"Disadvantages of human resource outsourcing

Less Control

When a company outsources their HR, they give up some control they would have if they kept their HR internal. When partnering with an outsourcing firm that doesn't understand the values and functions of a business, many business owners find it difficult to keep track of what's going on in that department. In order to combat this, when choosing an outsourced HR firm make sure they have a deep understanding of your industry and business values – they should be a cultural fit. Also, make sure you're able to communicate with them effectively. An HR firm should be partners, not just a company that is off in the distance that you talk to every few weeks.

Source:
https://www.milestone.inc/blog/outsourcing-and-its-hr-implications

Aside from these points, which have an awful lot of truth in them, the thing that needs to be remembered about any outsourced service is that they will, like any other business, always be looking to shave the cost of running the service to the customer.

Unfortunately, the tendency for large corporates to offshore their customer contact centres or reduce the number of client-facing personnel has led to an inevitable degradation of the service, dissatisfaction and eventually loss of business.

The customer experience is paramount more than ever today, and when the problems relate to employees, issues can get extremely personal and need sensitive handling which is not known to be a call-centre skill set.

The most famous outsourcing exercise in the HR world was in 1999, when **BP Amoco** passed most of its HR functions to the newly founded **Exult** consultancy in a $600 million ten-year deal.

In 2001, the company reported that it had saved $100 million dollars the previous year because of the outsourcing.

In *HRO Today* some years after, **Dirk Olin** was able to outline some of the setbacks encountered during the BP Amoco-Exult journey. Although BP terminated the arrangement a couple of years early, they went on to re-sign with Exult's new owners, **Hewitt**, two years after. Two years after the 2004 Exult acquisition, Hewitt had reported a net loss of $115.9 million, citing HR outsourcing as a contributor.

International Paper Co. (IP) also passed their US HR function to Exult. **HRO Today** reported on the learning curve that this type of deal demanded, and outlined some of the obstacles encountered, not least being the speed of change both within and outside of the client companies and their personnel.

2. HRO Today commented

"As the industry enters its second decade of major HR BPO, observers are taking stock. Call it the great sorting. Gone are naïve dreams of world-changing, end-to-end efficiencies and cost savings. Instead, HR practitioners are carefully weighing which functions can be farmed out (that is, which can essentially be commoditized) and which are so strategic that they should be held close for customization and configuration. Both sides would also do well to train a gimlet eye on adapting deals in real time."

Sources:
https://www.wsj.com/articles/SB945129749987949153
https://www.personneltoday.com/hr/bp-makes-100m-saving-since-handing-hr-to-exult/
https://www.hrotoday.com/news/sourcing/the-great-vendor-bender/
https://www.hrotoday.com/news/sourcing/as-deal-renewals-come-up-pioneers-reflect-on-learnings/

We always need to bear in mind that it is highly risky to try to outsource problems and complexity; the operation to be outsourced must be functioning as optimally as is possible before passing it to a third party.

When we read about the complexity of BP Amoco's payroll

and process operations, it's no wonder that the outsourcing company would struggle to economically deliver a fully functional service; the rationalisation project should have happened long before the handover.

In conclusion, outsourcing HR is not an easy decision, and if you decide to go that route you will need to prepare the way thoroughly and ensure that you devote the right resources to keep it running effectively.

Chapter Fifteen – Processes

An important part of any HR transformation is to re-examine the current work processes that affect the department. Regular reviews are necessary, as per the laws of inertia, too often a process becomes something "we've always done that way".

Process maps will give you important signposts as to if the flow is working optimally, especially if running digitally, as well as giving essential insight to the user experience; if this is poor, people will find ways to bypass the correct procedure.

I identify key processes for HR as being:

Recruitment initiation and fulfilment

Being the whole run between a vacancy being identified and approved, recruitment through own module sitting on your website or via third parties, interview planning, offers and acceptance.

Starters

Following on from recruitment, the stages from acceptance to on boarding a new employee.

Performance management

How the process is initiated, within what timelines the review must be completed, evaluation criteria, and reward or further action if appropriate. Identification of any developmental needs that may arise, and of course any benefits attached to performance.

Learning & Development

Ideally following on from a previous performance review, how an identified developmental need is approved and delivered, the timeline, cost and whether or not the required effect was brought about by the learning, thereby giving a Return-on-Investment calculation.

Transactional changes

Administrative actions and approvals for salary / position / department / reporting line or location changes.

Absence

How sickness is reported and recorded, holiday bookings and other absence types e.g.

maternity/paternity/adoption

sabbatical

jury or other obligatory public service

compassionate leave

unpaid leave

Employee Relations

All processes relating to the disciplinary, grievance and appeal procedures that are set down in the employee conditions, together with prescribed timelines and appropriate respondents. As a minimum, these must conform to legislative requirements.

Things can go very wrong if the company – often in the form of HR - doesn't stick to its own processes as happened in this case reported in **Personnel Management** in 2023.

https://www.peoplemanagement.co.uk/article/1813511/ factory-worker-victim-sex-discrimination-when-hr-took-female-colleagues-complaint-seriously-his-tribunal-rules

HR had reassured the complainant that her complaint would be "thoroughly reviewed" and asked her to keep her complaint a "secret". Meanwhile, a complaint by the other party was not formally acknowledged. At several other points along the way, there were failures in process.

A legal expert commented that *'the employer should have ensured there was a "robust grievance policy and procedure in place", and that regular training would ensure the process was followed. "Had the same process been followed for both employees, with equal time and attention given to their concerns and comparable action taken against each person, it's probable this case would have had a different outcome,"* he added. '

Another legal expert concluded that *"The lesson for employers is clear: ensure your policies are up to date and legally sound if you fail to follow them without reasonable explanation, it is open to an employee to draw adverse inferences under equality law,"*

Having policies is not enough; they need to be followed to the letter.

Leavers

How a leaver is processed from date of advice of termination until final day, to include exit interview procedure as well.

HR processes may vary from employer to employer, but the basic components are nearly always present.

A way to keep mapping exercises simple is to take a process and run a group session, with input coming from those involved, those affected by it, and a facilitator doubling as objective observer.

To visualise the processes, I personally like to use a white wall and Post-it© notes. Participants can identify each stage in the process and those responsible for it, the information being written on the sticky note and pegged to the wall.

The order of the notes is confirmed in the group, and the full process then reviewed for completeness and a sense check, and perhaps modification and finally produced as a map.

This is the moment to see if there are steps that are illogical or unnecessary but remember to get consensus on any changes before you put them into effect!

Do try to eliminate anomalies and exceptions, as these will only impede your process flow further on. To show how wasteful unchecked processes can be I will give a couple of real-life examples.

Example A
Holiday requests

No matter how you set up lines of authority, make sure that you build in defaults in the event of the first line of authority being absent; avoid what happened to a CEO once, who, returning from a business trip to the States, found his inbox full of holiday requests. Because the manager of one of the largest departments was away sick, and an alternative authority had not been specified, the system escalated the request to the highest point in the structure!

Authorisation levels need to be thought through. Where the chain of command is linear, this is straightforward, depending on whether you assign authority to the person or the post. In matrix structures, such as are found in projects and campaigns, there may be more than one authorising person.

Example B
Recruitment requests

In one company I knew of, seven authorisations were needed to hire a replacement staff member.

The Managing Director went out and hired a sales manager, and it took HR nearly a month to gather all the necessary signatures, that by then had no meaning.

You can validate processes by reproducing the steps on the process map using a current transaction of the same type, either manually or using an existing HR system, and then see if the result is the same.

What you may find is that different parts of the organisation use variations on the same process in which case you'll need to get acceptance for standardisation.

Avoid transferring your old processes unchecked on to a new HR system, or you will not be maximising the benefits of the enhanced technology.

Where you are introducing digital processes to an organisation, you need to not only consider the management of culture change, but every person with access to the HR system will need a defined level of security to read and/or change records and initiate actions. This is effectively done by defining security access using grade or functional necessity.

Chapter Sixteen – Redundancy

To my mind, every redundancy is a management failure. The first time anyone is made redundant, the impact is profound, and somehow there's never the same relationship between the employee and any other employer they work for.

I'm not going into the legal ramifications here, they are laid down to be followed and failure to do so will result in penalties. Rather, I want to focus on three aspects of what's been happening in recent times: the Why, Who and the How.

Since the end of the pandemic restrictions, wholesale cuts of jobs have been announced at regular intervals particularly by the larger tech companies such as Google, Salesforce and Microsoft, these decisions impacting thousands of employees around the world, but mostly in the USA.

Firstly, let's look at some of the reasons

Why

November 2022

On taking over **Twitter**, new owner **Elon Musk** announced that he would cut the number of employees (then around 7000) in half. Musk was "under pressure to find ways to slash costs of a business for which he says he overpaid. "said Fortune and said he wanted to focus on the core product. "Software engineering, server operations & design will rule the roost," he tweeted in October 2022.

Source:
https://fortune.com/2022/11/03/elon-musk-twitter-layoffs-half-all-jobs-3700-remote-work/

That same month **Meta** announced 11,000 job cuts, after a disastrous collapse in revenue has left the company behind Facebook overstaffed and *"inefficient"*, the CEO **Mark Zuckerberg said** in a note to staff.

He indicated that he would continue backing the company's controversial multibillion-dollar bet on virtual reality, saying the metaverse project was a *"high-priority growth area"*.

"Unfortunately, this did not play out the way I expected," he said. *"Not only has online commerce returned to prior trends but the macroeconomic downturn, increased competition, and ads signal loss have caused our revenue to be much lower than I'd expected. I got this wrong, and I take responsibility for that."*

In February 2023 there were rumours of further cuts on the way.

Sources:
Guardian Business Live Updates9th November 2022
https://www.forbes.com/sites/qai/2023/02/03/meta-rumored-to-make-further-layoffs-prompting-surprising-market-reaction/?sh=1230927816d1

January 2023

Sundar Pichai, CEO of **Google** and its parent company, **Alphabet,** announced that he was laying off 12,000 employees.

"Over the past two years we've seen periods of dramatic growth," Pichai wrote in an email to employees. *"To match and fuel that growth, we hired for a different economic reality than the one we face today."*

Same month, **Salesforce** announced a 10% cut in the workforce,with CEO and co-founder **Marc Benioff** explaining that the company had hired too many people during the pandemic. *"As our revenue accelerated through the pandemic, we hired too many people leading into this economic downturn we're now facing."*

Still in January 2023, German software company **SAP** said it planned to cut some 3,000 jobs this year saying it planned to carry out a *"targeted restructuring programme"* to *"strengthen its core business"* and improve efficiency.

Source:
https://www.ndtv.com/world-news/core-business-in-focus-software-giant-sap-to-lay-off-3-000-workers-3726093

And, yet again in that month **Amazon** announced around 18,000 job losses because, as CEO **Andy Jassy** explained, Amazon had *"hired rapidly over the last several years,"* but added that the layoffs will help the company *"pursue more long-term opportunities with a stronger cost structure."*

Sources:
https://www.aboutamazon.com/news/company-news/update-from-ceo-andy-jassy-on-role-eliminations

February 2023

Yahoo announced it would slash 20% of its workforce. **Yahoo** CEO **Jim Lanzone** stressed that the layoffs are not attributable to financial challenges, but rather, strategic changes to the company's Yahoo for Business advertising unit, which is not profitable.

"These changes will be "tremendously beneficial for the profitability of Yahoo overall," he said, which will allow the company *"to go on offense"* and invest more in other parts of its business that are profitable.

"…We believe these changes will simplify and strengthen our advertising business for the long run, while enabling Yahoo to deliver better value to our customers and partners," a

spokesperson told the BBC.

Sources:
https://www.bbc.com/news/technology-64596061
https://www.axios.com/2023/02/09/yahoo-layoffs-2023-tech-media-companies

The same month**, Zoom** CEO **Eric Yuan** announced 1300 job losses explaining that Zoom had had scaled up rapidly to manage the demand of the pandemic, tripling in size within 24 months. But he also acknowledged it didn't spend enough time assessing whether that growth was sustainable or *"toward the highest priorities."*

Source:
https://www.npr.org/2023/02/08/1155392099/zoom-layoffs-tech-jobs

If we look at the reasons for this selected batch of layoffs, there are three salient points that emerge:

1. The companies had scaled up their workforce in recent years, mainly to deal with pandemic conditions

2. The job cuts were to position the businesses for anticipated economic conditions

3. With one exception – Twitter – those businesses were still earning well.

The announcement of job cuts often leads to a surge of shareholder sentiment with a corresponding increment in share price, and so it was with Meta (5%) Google (6%) Amazon (15%) Meta (3.8%) Salesforce (3.2%) and Zoom (7%)

(various sources, mainly WSJ)

A useful part of executive pay and bonus packages involves share or other equity options, so we can now see a correlation between the sacrificing large numbers of employees and the improvement in executive reward, even though those job losses came about because of what can only be described as bad decision-making at the top.

Who

We have seen glimpses of ownership of responsibility in some of the statements making the announcements. **Jason Aten** Tech Columnist at **Inc.** nailed this apparent sackcloth and ashes approach in an article entitled *"**Google's CEO Said He Takes 'Full Responsibility' for Laying Off 12,000 People. Why That's Mostly Meaningless**

Responsibility without accountability doesn't mean what you think it does."

This article merits repetition here as it goes to the heart of what is currently going wrong.

"This brings me to the email from Sundar Pichai, CEO of Google and its parent company, Alphabet, which announced that he was laying off 12,000 employees. Pichai published his email to employees to the company's blog. Here's how it starts:

> *"I have some difficult news to share. We've decided to reduce our workforce by approximately 12,000 roles. We've already sent a separate email to employees in the U.S. who are affected. In other countries, this process will take longer due to local laws and practices.*
>
> *This will mean saying goodbye to some incredibly talented people we worked hard to hire and have loved working with. I'm deeply sorry for that. The fact that these changes will impact the lives of Googlers weighs heavily on me, and I take full responsibility for the decisions that led us here. "*

The problem is the last sentence. Pichai says that the decision «**weighs heavily on me**,*" which I'm sure is true. He then says that he takes* "**full responsibility for the decisions that led us here.**"

I'll explain why that's so problematic, but first, it's worth looking at what he means by the "decisions" he's talking about. Google, like a lot of companies, expanded rapidly during the pandemic. It added employees as its business grew, somehow never considering that when people are able to do things like go to restaurants and movie theaters again, they might not spend quite so much time online.

"Over the past two years we've seen periods of dramatic growth," Pichai wrote. "**To match and fuel that growth, we hired for a different economic reality than the one we face today**."

That's important. This isn't something that just happened to Google. It's the result of an intentional decision to spend money on hiring.

The other thing that's worth considering is that Google made almost $14 billion in profit in the most recent quarter it reported results. (Google has not announced its fourth quarter, or full-year earnings for 2022.) That›s the amount of money it made after paying everyone›s salary, which tells me it certainly could afford to keep those 12,000 people on the payroll if it wanted. Of course, that would not look good to Wall Street and investors if it continues to decline.

That leads me to why it's such a problem. Pichai says he "takes full responsibility," but responsibility without accountability is meaningless. **Pichai** isn't losing his job. Neither did **Satya Nadella** at **Microsoft**, or **Marc Benioff** at **Salesforce**, or **Mark Zuckerberg** at **Meta**.

In none of those cases was there anything that looks like accountability for the people who made the decisions that put their companies in a position where they had to lay off a large number of people. It wasn't the fault of the employees that their company grew too fast, or that its managers miscalculated the right strategy.

There are a variety of reasons why those CEOs aren't held accountable. In the case of Zuckerberg and Benioff, they are *founders who have effective control over their companies. With Pichai and Nadella, their overall performance as CEOs -- at least in terms of creating shareholder value -- means their boards aren't likely to ever hold them accountable.*

A good rule might be that if you are the CEO of a public company and you have to lay off more than one percent of your employees, your salary is automatically frozen for three years and you give up any stock earnings during that time. It's only reasonable that if you're trying to save expenses by letting go of that much staff, the CEO should share in that pain -- for real, not just with a blog post about having to make a "difficult decision." That's what taking "full responsibility" really means.

Sometimes layoffs seem like the best option, but it's important to remember that they don't happen because employees aren't doing their job. They happen because the CEO made a bet about the direction of the economy, and was wrong. It's always the employees who feel the most pain, but the leaders at the top should do more than take full responsibility. They should be held accountable."

Source:
https://www.inc.com/jason-aten/googles-ceo-said-he-takes-full-responsibility-for-laying-off-12000-people-why-thats-mostly-meaningless.html

Now contrast this with what happened at **Zoom**.

In the same **NPR** article quoted above, CEO **Eric Yuan** *"took responsibility for those mistakes and said he would "show accountability" by reducing his salary for the coming fiscal year by 98%, as well as forgoing his 2023 corporate bonus. Members of Zoom's executive leadership team will reduce their base salaries by 20% for the year and forfeit their corporate bonuses too, he added."*

Now that is truly shouldering blame and accepting a penalty. Of course, he is still in post, but at least he is not sailing serenely on, shedding crocodile tears. He is to be admired for this.

Finally we come to the **How** and HR professionals will have gone through, maybe several times over the course of a career.

In jurisdictions where there are employee safeguards, there are consultation periods, redundancy criteria, properly crafted severance packages and even after-care such as career advice.

Nothing however would prepare the workforce – and the world at large – for the grandstanding by Elon Musk at Twitter, who made a much-publicised and clumsily punned entrance to the offices and shortly after fired the CEO, the CFO and the Legal affairs & Policy Chief pretty much on the spot.

 Following on from that, about half of the staff were terminated and around 4000 contractors as well.

Later, employees who were cut received notice via emails entitled: *"Your Role at Twitter."*

"After further review of our workforce, we have identified roles within our organizational structure that are no longer necessary," the note reads, according to a copy seen by Bloomberg. *"Today is your last working day at the company."* The note, which goes on to explain that details on severance and returning company property are coming later, is signed, *"Twitter."*

Source:
https://www.latimes.com/business/story/2022-11-21/musk-fires-more-twitter-sales-workers-after-hardcore-purge

He then presented the remaining workforce with an ultimatum, to commit to a new "hardcore" company or leave with severance pay.

The distribution of job losses focused on divisions and the executive board rather than based on individual performance evaluations, which would suggest that a lot of talent was flitched from the workforce without due consideration.

In March 2022, **P&O Ferries** sacked around 800 employees without notice and replaced them with agency workers, which drew considerable public condemnation. Strictly speaking, this was not in itself illegal, but certainly not the standard of ethics one would expect of an employer. Many of the employees were only notified by a pre-recorded video message featuring the P&O Ferries HR director **Andy Goode.**

Methods of communication have varied among the large-scale lay offs.

Amazon began its layoff of 18,000 workers by informing them by email and cutting off their access to work computers: 'Unfortunately, your role has been eliminated'

Laid off **Google** workers in New York City who arrived at the office on Friday found that they could not enter the building as their badge access was cut off.

Over at **Salesforce** some affected employees learned of their firings through email and Slack.

"Email layoffs and no call from a manager. Unbelievable," wrote one impacted staffer.

"Unable to access Slack. Completely blindsided. I was on a finance all-hands call recently and no mention or hint from senior leadership," said another.

There seems to be a corporate disconnect somewhere. Benioff promised that *"[l]eadership will reach out directly to these employees, and provide clarity for their teams about changes within their organizations."*

Source:
Channel Futures 4 Jan 2023

Insult was added to injury when Benioff showed up 15 minutes late to an all-company meeting the day after announcing layoffs of around 10% of its staff. *"Did I miss something?"* he asked after the call's late start, the **Times of London** reported.

One person on the call told **The Times:** *"We knew more [layoffs] were coming, so we were all there to find out if we would still have jobs."*

"It was so inappropriate," they added. *"Employees were very,*

very upset."

At the end of 2021, **Vishal Garg**, CEO of **Better.com** fired around 900 of his staff on a single Zoom call.

"If you're on this call you're part of the unlucky group being laid off," he said.

"Last time I did [this] I cried," Mr Garg told the staff on the call.

"I wish the news were different. I wish we were thriving," he said. This time his tone was measured and he referred to notes on the desk in front of him.

Source:
https://www.bbc.com/news/business-59554585

And finally we come to the case of the 'Crying CEO', reported in the '**Guardian**' in August 2022.

*"**Braden Wallake** had a difficult choice to make. The 32-year-old CEO of **HyperSocial**, a marketing agency, had just sacked two of his 17 employees and needed to choose between quietly helping the newly unemployed pair move on with their lives and turning their misfortune into self-aggrandising online content.*

You've guessed it: Wallake chose option two.."

He posted a blubbing selfie on LinkedIn and the story went viral. Somehow, he had made it about him (still CEO and employed) instead of the two unfortunate departing employees.

https://www.theguardian.com/commentisfree/2022/aug/16/crying-ceo-sacked-two-people-selfie-linkedin

Let's be clear on this: Redundancy has to be carried out transparently; the right communication at the right time is essential, and no amount of handwringing is going to lessen the impact. These sackings – and that's what they are, not 'letting go' or any other euphemisms – must be conducted Humanly and Compliantly, with due prior consultation. Added to this must be Fair selection criteria, commensurate Compensation and Notice periods, and an offer of further Support to find alternative employment.

I close this section with some good advice given by **HRZone** about HR in any redundancy exercise:

"As HR professionals, our stewardship puts us at the heart and centre of helping to manage not just processes, but also emotions. HR's role is to maintain constant, consistent communication, whilst supporting the continuation of business priorities. We're in the middle. And of course, all whilst managing our own emotions at a time of uncertainty – bear in mind we may only know as much as the employees we represent and serve."

".. Here are some practical tips:

1. Be prepared

After all, redundancies aren't an everyday occurrence. Brush up on your knowledge and best practice on processes and be prepared for questions employees may have.

Consider what questions you might ask if you were in this position. And as a word of caution – don't try to answer a question you don't know the answer to. It's far better to be honest and say you don't know and will find out the answer later.

If you're a CIPD member, remember you can get additional benefits like employment law advice and access to wellbeing support if you need it.

It's ok to have your own worries and concerns – just don't bottle them up.

2. Don't let suspicious eyes impact your behaviour

Often, the relationship between HR and employees can change quickly when redundancies are proposed – suspicions arise that HR know more than they let on. It can be assumed that our agenda has changed from being a highly supportive function, to one who's role is now to make redundancies happen and save costs as quickly as possible – which is rarely the case.

Despite any possible change in opinion, continue to be your authentic self, and remember the reasons you came to work in

HR in the first place.

3. Be mindful of your own wellbeing

Practically, this might be updating your own CV and asking the questions you need some clarity on. Or maybe, wellbeing support to keep your mind on track, whilst continuing to support others. It's ok to have your own worries and concerns – just don't bottle them up. You need to be in a good headspace to help the employees you look after too.

4. Lead with integrity

Your sense of purpose is more important than ever through turbulent times. In the employment lifecycle and through a redundancy process, this challenge brings on the most testing of time. Despite any personal thoughts and challenges you may have, hold your head high and ensure your performance continues to be at its peak.

After all, whatever happens, and whenever any processes conclude, you never know who you'll meet on the HR road. Be positively and fondly remembered for how you treated others at a time of uncertainty and worry. It might just help you in your own future. "

Source:
https://www.hrzone.com/lead/change/how-should-hr-at-shell-energy-asda-and-royal-mail-navigate-the-redundancy-risk-period?utm_medium=email&utm_campaign=HRZTHUR090223&utm_content=HRZTHUR090223+CID_a8665efdf4854509bbdf1c6d290eab64&utm_source=internal_cm&utm_term=Four%20lessons

Chapter Seventeen – Succession Planning

Succession Planning has always been a cornerstone of HR beliefs but is it relevant to today's landscape?

At the top of the tree, when the big name departs, the shareholders usually clamour for a replacement from the perpetually-revolving Chief Executive carousel rather than opt for the heir/ess apparent, who then gets elbowed aside.

Let's not blind ourselves to the fact that the executive who has a successor warming up in the wings will want to burnish their legacy and do some grandstanding in the meantime or cling on to the trappings of power – and their benefits – for as long as possible.

If we can't practice what we preach at the top level, how can we make it work further down the food chain?

I can recall a case where an outgoing managing director appointed two successors splitting the role, apparently to emphasise that not one person could possibly replace him.

Even that guru of cost-cutting and job shedding **Jack Welch** wasn't immune to unnecessary extravagance at the end; he and **GE** agreed to a "retention package" worth $2.5 million, and which promised continued access after Welch's retirement to benefits he had received as CEO—including an apartment in New York, baseball tickets and the use of a private jet and chauffeured car. And he chose a successor who was never going to outshine him, and who turned out to be a failure.

The re-appearance of **Bob Iger** at **Disney** has a parallel in that the successor was a company man of long standing, and the succession failed.

If the anointed one is made to hang around too long, if they are any good at all they'll find plenty of takers happy to give them the top spot without delay – and thereby emerge from the shadow of the previous incumbent.

In a sense, that is the human problem with succession planning; if the plan is common knowledge, the chosen one then goes into a holding pattern. If they start trying to stretch their wings, they'll be reminded that they aren't in the chair just yet.

Gordon Brown's interminable wait for **Tony Blair** to stand aside as PM of the United Kingdom developed into a prolonged and somewhat distasteful countdown in public.

The most practical way to succession planning could be developed would be to skill up a group of people who show talent and ensure that you have a pool of candidates for senior posts when they become vacant.

Here too, lies another problem with succession; the post holder won't – or can't - move up or out when they maybe ought to. Too many directors and managers are sitting in jobs where they no longer make a difference and are in effect putting in the time needed to max the retirement or severance package.

Further down the ladder, the question of succession becomes easier, as in a departmental hierarchy, successors are easier to identify, usually by experience, but it is important that those 'pretenders' are upskilled not only in the technical aspects of the function, but also in how to manage people compliantly and effectively.

My view is also that modern structures and roles are becoming far more fluid, so without that rigidity it must make more sense to develop talents within the individual rather than grow them for a specific ladder of roles.

Personnel Today hinted as much in an article in January 2020:

"Succession planning often focuses on key leaders in the organisation. But in a changing business environment, planning for the future needs to be far more strategic and widespread"

And another strong point in the same article when they said that an organisation should know when to look externally:

"Sometimes, it's necessary to expand beyond your current team. Recognise that you might not have the skill sets, experience, diversity, and other criteria for the role(s) you need to fill. There may be valid reasons to conduct an external search, and bring in outside perspectives and skills, especially if there are gaps among your internal team. Additionally, external hires can help increase diversity within your organisation."

Source:
https://www.personneltoday.com/hr/is-succession-planning-an-outdated-concept/

Chapter Eighteen - A Seat in the Boardroom

This is probably the hottest HR topic and has been for quite a while! The Holy Grail for HR is a seat at the Boardroom table, but is it truly merited? And, just as importantly, what could they achieve by being there?

Most senior HR professionals as well as some outside observers believe that HR should be represented at Board level. Here are some of the commentaries that support that view:

TEC Canada re-published an article originally from the **Vistage Research Centre** entitled *'Why Your Business Should Give HR a Seat at the Table'*

1. *"...HR's potential has been undervalued, unappreciated, and underutilized through. Today, however, it's nearly impossible to achieve your goals without strategic human resource management. Holding on to outdated views of what HR should be and do can make your company less effective, less competitive, and less profitable. This, at a time when every*

organization's biggest challenge is top talent—including finding the people you need and keeping the people you have.

If you don't already have an outstanding chief human resources officer (CHRO), I hope you'll immediately seek one. Having a strategic human resource management leader on your team will ensure that you have a competitive edge in both winning and retaining the best people. You can't grow your business without them."

Note that here the emphasis is on recruitment and retention which in practice is more in the hands of line management. It continues

"The focus of strategic HR is less about serving the best interests of employees and more about harnessing and channelling human potential to benefit the business as a whole. Strategic HR still performs all of the more transactional responsibilities related to hiring, developing, and retaining employees. These tasks are inseparable from the human resources function. What is different is that strategic HR no longer works in a silo. "When it sets performance expectations, establishes rewards programs, or determines benefits, a strategic HR department works closely with other functional departments and outside advisors. Together, they make sure HR policies and programs are integrated with other business strategies."

We're back to perception here, as HR does not set performance or rewards and benefits. In our new mission, the function may establish frameworks for operating these activities, but is not the decision-maker.

"CHROs can earn a respected seat at the table by developing workforce programs and plans that solve business issues. As part of the executive team, they will directly contribute to a company's goals and profitability. A truly strategic HR serves as a supportive link between individual employees, teams, and departments—and is willingly and fully accountable for the quality of its decisions."

"…Your CHRO:

Takes a strategic and future-oriented point of view

Focuses on business results and your competitive advantage

Uses marketing expertise and perspective in creating and maintaining your employee brand

Emphasizes the candidate experience in the recruiting process

Concentrates on jobs and talent with the biggest business impact

Uses data rather than intuition for recruiting, learning, and predicting performance

Invests both internally and externally in strategies to win and keep people

Shows business acumen in the role of talent advisor"

Source:
https://tec-canada.com/insights/why-your-business-should-give-hr-a-seat-at-the-table/

Although these statements are moving broadly in the right direction, there is no demonstrable direct line of sight between the CHRO role and business effectiveness. Some of the attributes in this CHRO list certainly don't convince me, as 'marketing expertise and perspective' and 'shows business acumen' aren't usually pre-requisites for recruiting into HR, are not easily measurable and aren't things you're likely to find in the required examination texts.

Of course, an exceptional HR Head will have all of these and more, and certainly would be expected to move on up and out of HR when the right opportunity presents itself.

Other reasons for HR to merit a seat on the board were outlined in **Morgan Latif's** blog of May 2020:

" HR leaders are business leaders

HR leaders are best placed to prepare workplaces for the future

HR leaders help organisations win the "war for talent"

HR leaders drive positive change

HR leaders are effective crisis managers"

They go on to give some ideas on how HR leaders can reach Board level:

"Seek out CEO roles in smaller organisations

Work in other business functions

Gain greater business knowledge

Be more vocal

Think more strategically about your network"

Source: https://morganlatif.com/resources/why-hr-leaders-deserve-a-seat-on-the-board

When we looked at HR People in Chapter Three, I laid emphasis on getting to understand the business, and gain background in other functions. This goes a long way to winning trust and credibility.

Working on a locum contract for a District Council once, I made a point of meeting department heads in every one of the many departments and talking about their issues. The Head of Housing said to me: "Goodness! It must be a couple of years since we saw an HR person down here!" Light-hearted, maybe, but with more than a grain of truth; HR was insulated in their own zone unless it was to appear and sit in on all the job interviews.

Talent Growth Advisors in January 2015 gave four reasons why HR doesn't have a seat at the table despite all its 'complaining' and I have included the sections which have relevance.

"Lack of HR Credibility

Many corporations have few, if any, strategic positions dedicated to HR. The demands placed on HR aren't financial or analytical in nature because companies don't position the function as such. Overwhelmed with personnel-related administrative responsibilities - and few demands tied to strategy or measurement - individuals in HR roles are viewed as having low "authority." In turn, this causes them to struggle establishing credibility, assessing strategic opportunities, and driving results-based change.

A Support Function Mindset

When jobs are tactical in nature, they appeal to people who like tactical work. Many HR professionals, when surveyed, report a preference for administrative, nonstrategic work. They often have a low tolerance for risk and a limited sense of what they care to "own" or have authority over. Studies such as **New Talent Management Network's 2013 State of Talent Managers Report** indicate that HR professionals have a lack of confidence in their own skills and abilities, which leads (in general) to choosing administrative work over more strategic, analytical career opportunities. It's not a leap to tie these results and conclusions to another data point: Only 32% of HR leaders have high confidence in their own strategy or actions

Skill and Capability Gaps

"Here is where it all comes full-circle. Nonstrategic, administrative jobs attract tactical-minded people who prefer more rote, task-driven work. Couple this with the bona fide difficulty of obtaining accurate, people-related data (that is, measurements related to quality of hire, cost of attrition, ROI of learning investments, and so on) and you've got a lack of data-based decision-making and forecasting that impedes the driving of change. These leaders are unable to gather and use data to create business cases and, in turn, build a 'burning platform' for significant changes or investments in their company's talent strategy."

Limited Aspirations"

To further illustrate the reason HR lacks strategic leadership and analytical skills, consider these other findings from the '**State of Talent Managers Report**':

"Most HR incumbents are in the function because they want to help people.

Only 18% aspire to be CHROs.

Sixty-eight percent consider themselves to be "top performers" yet . . .

Sixty-nine percent stated they have only a "slight" understanding of their company's business."

A major failing of HR was reckoned to be:

"HR's... inability to measure their plans and efforts. In turn, (this) hampers companies' efforts to measure the effectiveness of their talent investments. Think about it: what other part of the business allows enormous investments of any kind (e.g., in equipment, technology, etc.) without a detailed business case, including the predicted return on the investment, and a robust debate about the need and possible solutions.

"Yet every day, companies sink untold dollars in hiring, training, retention and engagement efforts without any expectation that such investments will be objectively and meaningfully evaluated."

Source:
https://talentgrowthadvisors.com/resources/blog/hr-seat-at-the-table

John Hooley, then HR operations manager at Windsor Lea Associates was particularly forthright in his views in **Personnel Today, May 2006** (unedited):

"I have observed in a totally unbiased manner a number of HR directors and, in general, they offer very little value to the worth of a company...

Occasionally, the odd one may be more strategic here and there – ie, they may have prepared a strategy to cut back on excessive agency fees, or have developed ideas that enable their company to avoid draconian headhunting costs. They may also have developed policies and procedures that can compliment (sic) their organisations' business.

Very few that I have ever seen or heard of add any real value. With some exceptions, they have mainly become buffers between operational management and corporate management.

Marketing directors are the root of a company and bring in business, which is the lifeblood. Good finance directors control the flow of finances and can have a truly stabilising effect.

HR directors can perform for the real benefit of a company and its employees. But they need to show this by motivating, leading and coming up with positive business ideas. That will gain the approbation of corporate management at board level that most in HR currently do not deserve."

Source:
https://www.personneltoday.com/hr/hr-directors-dont-deserve-a-seat-in-the-boardroom/

We should note that not all businesses have felt the need for HR. **Greg Jackson** is the founder and CEO of **Octopus Energy**, a UK start-up valued at more than £1.4bn ($2bn), selling green energy.

"Despite now having more than 1,200 employees, he says he has no interest in traditional things like human resources (HR) and information technology (IT) departments.

There is a tendency for large companies to "infantilise" their employees and "drown creative people in process and bureaucracy", says Jackson.

HR and IT departments don't make employees happier or more productive in his experience, he says."

Source:
https://www.bbc.com/news/business-56130187

A valued colleague, Charles Fiddes Payne points out that in organisations such as consultancies whose only real asset is "the expertise in the heads of their employees, would benefit from HR's planning, influencing, and enabling...In such organisations, an HR professional could legitimately become CEO."

"Then there are organisations wherein iterable process in a stable organisational structure is what they have to sell, where the process is very people-heavy, e.g. service providers - would HR not be critical *to their success?"*

Note that these types of business are where career progression to HR Director is very possible.

"Then there are the organisations wherein Intellectual Property is critical to success, because IP goes out of the door when the em-

ployees do."

"All of these groups have one thing in common - the only way to increase productivity is through design intelligence, improving the knowledge, creativity, and efficiency of how goods & services are created & delivered, and that's entirely a human thing, not a finance or a tech, or a logistics, or a whatever thing. These organisations require HR on the Exec. Board."

Conclusion

My overall view is that there should be no automatic entitlement for the HR function to have a seat on the Board, except where the business demands it or where the Head of HR is exceptional, understands the business, can enable it to perform better and is able to communicate overall at the highest level on key business issues – and formulate solutions.

Chapter Nineteen- Time to Lose the HR Handle

The function needs a new title to reflect its changed mission. The jokes about 'Human remains' and 'Hardly relevant' have been done *ad nauseam* and are so over by now. As I mentioned at the beginning of this book, we have transitioned from what was essentially a welfare function to what aspires to be a fully-fledged business activity.

To match these aspirations, the titles became harder-sounding - there was a flurry of support for the chilly term 'Human Capital' that was originally coined in the 1960s, but one rarely hears it now in the company of anyone with a pulse - and have now segued into the more ethereal to match the more allegedly 'laid back' working environments. So now we have Chief Happiness Officers amongst others.

What is growing all the time is the word 'People' applied to anything in HR territory, as in 'Head of People' and 'People Director' or even 'People and Culture'

BambooHR in their *'The State of Human Resources Leadership es*

*Leadership Report (2023 Data)' asked **"Is a "Human Resources" Title Out of Date?"***

"One of the most popular choices is a title featuring "People," such as Chief People Officer. Nearly 2 in 5 HR managers at startups (39%) currently or previously have used a "People" title."

"Some other human resource titles used by companies in our report include:

Chief Colleague Experience Officer

Head of Human Capital Management

VP of Talent

Chief of Staff

VP of Employee Success"

To my mind, any of the 'People' titles are misleading, as they give the impression that the people in the organisation are in their charge, whereas the only people that they actually have any authority over are HR people.

Whatever the new moniker is going to be I'll leave for others to decide and hope they choose something meaningful. My personal vote would be for **Workforce Enablement**; I saw that in someone's job title and rather liked it. **WE** could be **<u>us</u>** one day!

MISSION: HR

PART FOUR – ACTION

Summary

In this section, I give some steer to where HR should be concentrating its resources.

If you're a newly appointed HR head, you'll have plenty of leeway during your 'halo' period, so you'll have a natural advantage over someone who is already established in post trying to turn the ship around.

There is no prescribed order to this, but I would tend to put in the technology for information purposes and devote energy in getting the line management trained up in compliance, ethical recruitment, and refreshers in managing people. These steps alone will save you work and problems further along.

Chapter Twenty –How?

Thinking positively, what can HR be doing that can truly make a difference?

For starters, HR needs to assume three key roles: Planner, Influencer and Enabler.

Planner: develop a clear blueprint for the function of what it does, how it does it and what the result should be.

Influencer: Gaining acceptance of the new plan across all levels of the organisation, all of which are essential for successful operation.

Enabler: executing all elements of the plan and keeping progress under continual review for improvement.

Let's look at the areas where we need to begin to execute our new mission. I list them as:

1. **Technology**
2. **Workforce Development**
3. **Compliance**

4. Organisational Aspirations (and Obligations)

5. Performance

6. Compensation

This is quite a broad front to operate across, but your first move is to outline your plan to the Board and get their approval. To do this you will emphasise the following advantages:

Technology – reduced administration, fewer errors, less wasted time, relevant information available to management.

Workforce Development – improving performance right across the board, together with better management reducing employee grievances.

Compliance – Operating in the correct manner, reduction of legal risk.

Organisational Aspirations (and Obligations) – building a visibly fair working culture where all talent is recognised. Less risk, better optics for recruitment (and retention).

Performance – A series of measures that directly relate back to output and task completion. Only with meaningful performance measures can the organisation assess how well it is doing.

Compensation – Fair reward for performance. Good for recruitment and retention.

Establish line-of-sight measures for all these activities and add in measures for the HR function at the same time! Now is the time that HR finally defines itself within the organisation.

Actions for the mission:

1. Technology

The first step is to make your HR software fit for purpose. Not only is that going to simplify much of the work ahead, but as we see in the Three Basic Laws of HR Tech, it is vital that workforce information is always available to management, and that demands good software and fully accurate data.

If you haven't got a system, you're going to need one unless you're small enough to manage with spreadsheets, and if you do have one but it's not working for you, then change it as soon as is possible.

The main elements of this are shown in **Appendix 3**

Sourcing the right HR software is a complete project *per se* and has been dealt with by me in considerable detail in another publication '***Selecting & Implementing HR & payroll software***'

It's a hard task, and needs to be done right, but the benefits you will reap are immense, and will lend real credibility in the function's ability to execute and deliver.

There are other elements of HR technology that you should consider deploying for safer and more effective working in today's business climate:

Wellness

In March 2021, **Bhagyashree Pancholy**, a top international tech lawyer, and I authored an article entitled '**How HR can use tech to support employees rather than watch them**'

In it we argued for a change of emphasis where passive surveillance is replaced by active engagement, looking after employees by ensuring that they take breaks and restricting excessive access to business systems outside of contracted hours except by logged requests. This can easily be done via the system security module.

> *Source:*
>
> *https://www.personneltoday.com/hr/how-hr-can-use-tech-to-support-employees-rather-than-watch-them/*

The most exciting developments in employee wellness have come from the support offered by specialist software platforms

Speakfully (www.speakfully.com) – a part of **HR Acuity**, provides a platform where employees can anonymously document their experiences and submit the details to company or external personnel authorised to deal with their issue. Employers receive real-time data and analytics through submitted reports, feedback left, and pulse survey results.

Humaxa (www.humaxa.com), where **"Max"** - a digital assistant chats with employees about the workplace, offers to help, and delivers insights to discreet support resources.

These technologies act as monitors to quickly bring problems into sharp focus before they escalate and give indicators of where help is needed.

They are invaluable not only in helping to protect employees from burnout, depression and even bullying or harassment, but make sense for employers wanting to do the right thing as well as reduce the probability of costly legal claims. The technology exists, it's out there, and it needs to be used now.

Team working

If you don't already have one, then you should invest in a tool for use by your various departments (e.g., Slack, MS Teams) irrespective of where they are located. That way your working groups stay connected and can access common resources.

Automation & Artificial Intelligence (AI)

Most HR systems offer basic levels of Automation, but there's always a use for more! Source an automation application that will enable you to do that by integrating with your HR system and giving you options to build automated processes. If your HR system is a legacy one, adding a suitable automation module can extend its useful life.

Automation is not about headcount reduction; it's about using technology to eliminate routine work seamlessly.

Many HR colleagues are getting excited about Artificial Intelligence (AI).

My view is that as a profession, we're still getting to grips with what I call linear systems, so let's not run before we can walk.

The logical steps are first to install Automation and then AI. But is AI necessary for the average organisation? Its advocates say that it can be used to predict who is most likely to leave the company. I'd rather invest the cash in managers who don't let that happen in the first place.

To those who say that AI will indicate the best candidates for recruitment, I would say that good managers can do that just as well. And if you have an undetected bias in your organisation that bias is more likely to be replicated in the AI recruitment processes.

You'll need to balance out purpose against likely cost and expertise required to make it work for you. Artificial Intelligence adopted too early could put you at the mercy of expensive programmers. I prefer to think of AI as a 24/7 'sentinel', monitoring data and data trends from within the system and giving alerts about matters that have been determined to be of importance.

In summary, I'm not saying that HR must be at the 'cutting edge' of technology, but rather be aware of what is proven and available to fulfil our tasks of putting measures in place to protect the organisation and its employee, giving the tools to allow it to carry on effectively regardless of what is happening outside in the world outside and to provide access to the data needed to make quality decisions.

2. Workforce Development

This will break into the following types of activity:

a) Line management development

Strong line management not only reinforces the senior team but makes for good HR as better-quality management reduces the number of unnecessary employee grievances and disputes.

Encourage your line manager to take a more Mentoring approach and use more Observation on how their teams tackle the tasks in hand.

b) Employee development

This has several strands, starting with Induction and the 'company way' of doing things. This should include both ethical and inclusive approaches that reflect the employer's culture.

Familiarisation with all policies and procedures, rights and obligations is essential, to give total transparency.

Compliance-related training such as e.g. first aider certificate or fire officer training.

Areas for performance improvement or enhancement identified by reviews. This is about enabling your employees to perform better by giving them the skills to do so.

Professional studies for relevant career tracks. Where possible, employees should be able to study for qualifications that will not only enable them to do more advanced work but adds to the company's skills capital as well.

Development for management potential. Managers should be able to spot employees with future leadership potential, and nominate these candidates for development, *once it is proven they have that capacity.*

The investment made in these initiatives needs to be monitored for value and effectiveness, by measuring tangible improvements over time.

3. Compliance

Check that your organisation is compliant with legal obligations, contractual and procedural across the spectrum of employee relations, ensuring that employer and employees are fully aware of legal rights and responsibilities. If employment law isn't your HR department's forte, don't dabble - get professionals in.

4. Facilitate organisational aspirations

Make sure that the company truly supports initiatives such as DEI, pay gap monitoring and elimination of bias throughout, and make sure this message, reinforced by the Board, goes out loud and clear.

Also with Board backing, encourage the workforce to suggest process or other improvements that can be implemented; reward these ideas if it makes them flow faster! Don't always rush to hire consultants for your solutions– ask the people who are working with the problem.

5. Performance

Examine all current performance measures for relevance and practicability; for this you will need to work closely with all other functions in the business and be prepared question the status quo. Once the agreed measures are in place, and a timetable for them being introduced, make sure that they are transparent to the management and workforce, and that progress is able to be monitored through the system, at a personal as well as departmental and divisional level.

6. Compensation

Frame packages within the organisational business plan that effectively reward performance across all functions, can compare favourably with other local or industry competition and present an attractive proposition to potential recruits.

These are high value activities that we should engaged on to build an HR function that has relevance. Have a look at your HR department and see how much of that is being done, as well as what they shouldn't be doing.

MISSION: HR

PART FIVE – THE FUTURE

Chapter Twenty-One -Epilogue

The last few years have generated a deluge of 'Future of Work' specialists, mainly due to repercussions of the pandemic. Managements generally started off trying to do the 'right thing' – because otherwise they found difficulty in recruiting good people - and then wobbled back to the traditional ways when they felt emboldened by market conditions tilting in their favour.

Whatever happens from now onwards, I don't think employees will ever have quite the same reverence towards Work and Employers. They had time and space out of the commuting rat race to really think about their lives and discovered that Work wasn't the Be All and End All of our existences.

The weaselly phrase 'Quiet Quitting' was coined by the Old Guard to describe the phenomenon of people doing what they were paid to do. Extra unpaid work was deemed to be necessary for career advancement and demonstrating loyalty; loyalty that was never reciprocated when managements needed to trim numbers to make bonus.

Technology has yet to make an even bigger impact on working life, so stand by for some dramatic changes. Bots such as Chat GPT, Google Bard and Jasper are changing the landscape faster than we know. Thus far, at least, I can assure you I am writing this in person right now!

HR Exchange published an article by **Francesca di Meglio** in its newsletter of 31ˢᵗ January 2023 '*9 HR Jobs ChatGPT Says It Can Do*' and I recommend my fellow professionals to look at these very carefully.

These were the headers:

Recruiting and Hiring

Onboarding

Employee Engagement

Performance Evaluation

Learning and development

Compliance and Policy

HR Data Management

Employee Assistance

Diversity and Inclusion

Source:
https://www.hrexchangenetwork.com/hr-talent-management/articles/9-hr-jobs-chatgpt-says-it-can-do

We have already touched on a couple of these in Employee

Wellness and Compliance, but I can see definite gains in other areas.

As a result, I see far more de-centralisation of the workforce management and enablement, even down to some elements being self-managing. This will most likely take off in start-ups who don't have traditional cultures and attitudes to overcome.

HR as a function will probably in time break up into a series of specialist activities as in its current form it doesn't really deliver the goods. I think newer groupings and associations will arise to challenge the established institutions and give a new lead and direction to the profession.

In these pages, I have given what I feel to be the foundations of what HR professionals should be prioritising; the next chapters are very much for them to write, and I wish them the very best of success in their efforts.

APPENDIX

1.*A **business Intelligence module** is a reporting platform that gathers data from one or more sources – in our case the HR system database - to present required intelligence and insights in report or dashboard format.

2.***The Three Laws**:

"HR will take responsibility to ensure that their organisation has an HR system configurable to meet its process and information needs."

"HR will be responsible for the accuracy and timeliness of information held in the system, providing a single source of truth and real-time reporting."

"HR system information will be freely available and in required formats to all in the organisation authorised to have access to this information."

3.***Technology**

The main elements you will almost certainly require are:

a) HR

The nucleus of this is the HR Database which contains all the fields relating to Personal data, Job, Reward, Diversity / Equity / Inclusion and so on.

The HR module should have the following features and functions as standard to give a wide range of options:

Absence

Collects and aggregates information on attendance, holidays, sickness, and other absences.

Notifications

These are advisory messages triggered by changes in specified data fields. These responses can take the form of email or SMS alerts.

Organisation charting

These are graphical representations of the organisational structure based on the hierarchies held in the database.

Performance

Configurable to replicate the organisation's own KPIs or Targets and achievements against those benchmarks

Self Service

Providing employees with access to the personal part of their records and the facility to change or modify them as well as self-reporting for sickness.

Layers of security within the function permit managers to view records and requests relating to their staff or departments.

Workflow and other Automation.

The automation of business processes, in whole or part, by which documents, information or tasks are passed from one participant to another or more for action, according to a set of procedural rules.

b) PAYROLL

Calculates Pay and Deductions and captures Insurance, Tax and Pension information for statutory use. Provides payslips and other benefit-related output. Every employer needs a reliable payroll.

c) RECRUITMENT

Automates much of the Recruitment process, including responses to candidates and Interview scheduling. Most offer the chance to use your own website or source from regular media and job boards.

d) LEARNING & DEVELOPMENT

Using a more advanced application than the conventional training administration module, L&D activity is in response to plugging gaps identified in performance reviews, tracking professional progress, anticipating future developmental requirements, and keeping tabs on the top talent you have in the organisation.

e) TIME & ATTENDANCE

Primarily deployed in production or manufacturing locations and gaining usage with the rise of remote and hybrid working, this software records employee attendance by "clocking" them in and out by a variety of means

Shift or working patterns can be allocated to groups or individuals which is invaluable for workforce planning. T&A systems also provide powerful reporting tools for a range of production statistics.

www.ingramcontent.com/pod-product-compliance
Lightning Source LLC
Chambersburg PA
CBHW060844220526
45466CB00003B/1239